HIKING THE WILDERNESS

A Backpacking Guide to the Wheeler Peak, Pecos, and San Pedro Parks Wilderness Areas

By Kay Matthews

ACEQUIA MADRE

P·R·E·S·S
P.O. Box 493
Placitas, New Mexico 87043

First Edition

ISBN 0-940875-02-0

TABLE OF CONTENTS

"Recreational development is not a job of building roads into lovely country but of building receptivity into the still unlovely mind."

—Aldo Leopold

Dedicated to all my hiking *compadres*—Marion, Nancy, Marcos, Jan, Stephanie, Mary and Rico—but especially to Mark and Jakob, for their grace and determination in the eye of the storm.

Special thanks to my sister Riki for her help with the manuscript.

INTRODUCTION

I grew up in Colorado, home to 54 of North America's 60 mountain peaks over 14,000 feet in elevation. You can't find much more rugged terrain than that, at least in our contiguous 48 states. However, when I discovered New Mexico, a different type of appreciation was awakened in me by the juxtaposition of both rugged mountain terrain and high desert mesa—a combination that makes this state unique. A diversity of people and lifestyles adds to its charm, and I became a New Mexico devotee and fervent admirer. Here is where I first walked the high mountain trails with a 40-pound pack and scrambled up the ancient Anasazi stairwells in the blistering Chaco Canyon heat. In New Mexico I learned to use my feet and lungs for something much more profound than pushing a gas pedal and screaming at lousy drivers. By profound I mean seeing, experiencing and being in a way that is made possible only by pushing yourself up a 10-mile trail to a stunningly beautiful alpine lake, stopping to admire the complexities of the fairy slipper orchid growing by the trail, or meeting a bear, in the wild, for the first time. New Mexico turns us all into believers sooner or later by the nature of its very real enchantment, however hackneyed that state slogan has become.

This book is for those who want to reaffirm their commitment that there is more to life than cars, jobs, stress and anxiety, those who want to know the sky, the stars, the sun and the wilderness. While there are many other hiking areas in the state, these wilderness areas offer extensive trail systems in a contained area and afford the hiker the best opportunity to experience diverse terrain, lengthy hikes, and that most precious commodity—solitude. These lands, designated wilderness by the authority of the 1964 Wilderness Act, are, by definition, the closest thing we have to "unspoiled" lands or "untrammeled" lands, where man is a "visitor only." As you read through the descriptions of each wilderness area, you will see that much of this land has, in the past, been "trammeled" by loggers, miners, grazers, etc., but the important thing to remember is that the wilderness designation insures that these lands are preserved for the future, that they are protected from further degradation, and maintained in as natural a state as possible. This is especially important in a wilderness such as the

Sandia Mountain Wilderness, backyard to a metropolis of close to 400,000 people, where the pressures an urban population can bring to bear are great.

Approximately 700,000 acres of land in New Mexico are classified wilderness, with many thousands more acres, both in the National Forest and Bureau of Land Management, still under consideration for that designation. While it represents a very small percentage of total forest lands in the state, we are lucky that each of our national forests contains at least one wilderness area. The far-flung Cibola National Forest administers the Apache Kid and Withington wildernesses in the Magdalena Ranger District, while the Manzano Mountain Wilderness and the Sandia Mountain Wilderness preserve the two mountain ranges near Albuquerque. To the north, Santa Fe National Forest contains the San Pedro Parks Wilderness in the San Pedro Mountains and the Pecos Wilderness in the Sangre de Cristo range. Carson National Forest, the northernmost of the state's forests, administers the Wheeler Peak Wilderness near Taos and the Latir Peak Wilderness northeast of Questa. In the southwestern part of the state lies the largest of the wilderness areas, the vast Gila Wilderness, adjacent to the Aldo Leopold Wilderness, both administered by Gila National Forest. To the southeast, the White Mountain and Capitan Wildernesses are administered by the Lincoln National Forest. The wilderness areas described in the ensuing chapters are the northernmost of New Mexico's wildernesses: Wheeler Peak, Pecos, and San Pedro Parks. Most of the trails in each wilderness are included, and a map of each wilderness area accompanies the text.

Section I. General Information

LIFE ZONES

Hiking in the wilderness areas of New Mexico is like taking a trip in land like that of the Sonoran desert of Mexico to that of the alpine tundra of Canada. Each climate, or life zone, is identified by elevation, exposure, latitude, and prevailing weather patterns. New Mexico hikes often begin in what is called the Upper Sonoran life zone, generally found at 6,500 to 7,500 feet in elevation, a climate hot in the summer time while mild in the winter. The sparse vegetation includes the ubiquitous Rocky Mountain juniper and the piñon pine, the decorative chamisa, Apache plume, chokecherry, gambel oak, and the cottonwood and box elder, which usually denote a spring. In the summertime, these Upper Sonoran springs are the first to dry up, so if your hike remains in this life zone, be sure to carry an adequate supply of water. The array of wildflowers includes the milkvetch and rockcress of springtime, the globemallow, coneflower, and wild buckwheat of fall.

Animals, especially birds and rodents, are abundant in this life zone. While you will probably not see many of them on your hike, this zone is home to pocket mice, Kangaroo rats, prairie dogs, ground squirrels, coyotes, foxes, rattlesnakes, king snakes, lizards, mule deer, mountain lions, and Rocky Mountain bighorn sheep. The latter two species, once hunted to near extinction and reintroduced in several areas of the state, remain low in population and vulnerable to manmade pressures such as habitat intrusion and illegal hunting. The bighorn herds, reintroduced into the Sandias in the 1940s, once swelled to over 300, but are now reduced to only a few sheep.

As you enter the Transition life zone (7,500 to 8,200 feet), the piñon-juniper vegetation begins to give way to the stately ponderosa pine, easily recognized by the reddish bark of the more mature trees and the distinctive smell of vanilla emanating from the trunk. Here the climate is slightly cooler and wetter than the Upper Sonoran. Other trees and bushes include the limber pine (named for its soft, pliant limbs), New Mexico locust, gray oak, hoptree, mountain mahogany, wild rose, and buckthorn. In the upper reaches of the Transition zone, the aspen and Rocky Mountain maple color fall hiking days yellow and red. In meadows and along stream banks bloom water hemlock, cinquefoil, redosier dogwood, and valerian. Pink phlox, western wallflower, and green gentian (deer's ears) grow in the dry, sandy soil. Many of the same species of animals found in the Upper Sonoran zone also live in the Transition life zone. I've seen rattlesnakes as high as 9,000 feet, and the larger mammal species such as sheep and deer travel through both zones. Here you will also see the Abert squirrel with its famous tufted ears, and perhaps an elusive red fox or bobcat.

The Canadian zone, between 8,200 and 10,000 feet, is where you begin to experience the "high country" feeling. Thick stands of Douglas fir, white fir, Engelmann spruce, and blue spruce create a sense of the forest primeval. Mountain meadows are dotted with clusters of aspen and carpeted with larkspur, columbine, fireweed, gentian, osha, geraniums, and bluebells. Here, summertime populations of mule deer, white-tailed deer (found more in the southern part of the state), Rocky Mountain bighorn sheep, and elk graze. Black bears, the biggest New Mexico carnivores, are still abundant in most forests. Their signs—scratch marks high up on aspen trees and torn up trail signs—are common in all the wilderness areas, and I've encountered the backside of a bear turning tail to run at the first sight of me. Beaver dams are evident in some of the mountain streams and lakes, although the creatures themselves, largely nocturnal, are elusive. Over a period of two years we witnessed the incredible industriousness of these builders as they felled an entire mountainside of aspen, creating a huge lake full of mounds and logs across a moderate size stream.

The Hudsonian zone is found at 10,000 to 12,500 feet in elevation. The more homogeneous vegetation is exposed to the harsh weather conditions similar to that of the Hudson Bay area to the north. Here grow the Engelmann spruce, cork bark fir, white fir, and aspen. If you're planning on making camp in this life zone, be prepared with a good waterproof tent, as summer rain storms create a cool, wet environment. Many of the same wildflowers of the Canadian zone grow here, along with Rocky Mountain iris, primrose, monkshood, and the fairy slipper orchid.

Living among the talus slopes of this region are the sometimes shy, sometimes emboldened marmot and pika. The larger, fat marmots, like to sun themselves on the rocks during the day while they nibble on grasses and keep an alert eye on hikers. Don't let their somnambulant behavior fool you, however, as one Wheeler Peak marmot managed to steal our lunch, consuming our cheese and pickles while we were taking a walk around an alpine lake.

The Alpine zone is where the tree line stops above 12,500 feet. Here, weather conditions are so severe that only low growing plants and flowers can survive. New Mexico has only a few peaks this high, and climbing the year-round snow covered peaks can be quite challenging. Many wildflowers bloom throughout the summer, though, turning the barren rock and tundra into a carpet of color: parry primrose, anemone, goldenrod, moss silene, stonecrop, buttercup and parry gentian proliferate.

Upper Sonoran life zone to the snow-capped Pecos peaks

PREPARATION

This section will focus on backpacking in the wilderness, although many of the wilderness trails are accessible for day hikes too. But the backcountry implies just that—remote, isolated areas that offer the hiker willing to carry a 40-pound pack the wilderness experience that a day hike cannot: few or no other people, abundant wildlife, rugged terrain, and a heightened sense of being that only wildness can elicit. So in this chapter, I will discuss planning a backpack trip, including basic equipment, meal preparation, water supplies, wilderness etiquette, etc. Usually the best way to initiate yourself into the fun of backpacking is to go with a friend who has some experience. Or sign up for a class or expedition sponsored by the Mountain Club, Sierra Club or other conservation association. But don't be intimidated by the thought of going out with some other neophytes. As long as you plan your trip carefully and your equipment and supplies are adequate, common sense will ensure that your trip turns out to be a good experience. And the rewards of a successful first backpacking venture are immeasurable.

Planning

Figure out exactly what kind of trip you want. If this is your first time out, you may want to stay only one or two nights on the trail. And you may want to cover fairly easy terrain while you're discovering how you fare with a 30 or 40-pound pack on your back. To find such a hike, talk to other backpackers about where they have been, get the maps of the areas you're considering to see what the elevation gains are, contact the local Forest Service ranger stations for their recommendations, or read some books like this one where the hikes are rated for their degree of difficulty.

Also take into account the time of year in which you plan to camp and the life zone you're interested in visiting. If it's late July or August and you want to see Johnson Lake in the Pecos or Lost Lake in Wheeler, you can count on seeing them in the rain. If you're well prepared, with a tent, rain gear, and waterproof boots, you can also count on seeing a plethora of wildflowers, lush alpine vegetation, and hopefully some rainbow trout on the end of your fishing line. Conversely, if you want to take a hike into Bandelier National Monument to the wilderness ruins, think about going in May or October, before and after the scorching heat of summer turns this Upper Sonoran hike into an inferno.

Water availability is one of the primary considerations in choosing your route. At two pounds per quart, it is one of the heaviest items you will have to carry and, consequently, will determine how far you can walk without replenishing your supply. Most high country hikes will be in areas where springs, streams, and lakes are plentiful (not necessarily so in the Cibola National Forest wildernesses, however). Here, you need carry only as much water as you need to reach the first water source (exactly how much water you need—and how to treat it—is discussed in the section WATER CONTAINERS AND PURIFIERS). In the lower life zones, where springs and creeks dry up quickly in the summer heat, you may have to plan on carrying all your own water and shorten your trip accordingly.

A cardinal rule of hiking, be it day hiking or backpacking, is to let someone at home know where you are going and when you plan to return. Even if you are hiking with a group of people, you should leave your itinerary, the names and addresses of the people in your group, and your car description and license number. If you or your group fail to show up within a reasonable amount of time, your friend can notify the State Police, who coordinate search and rescue operations. If at all possible, follow your planned itinerary so that if you do become lost or hurt, the search team will know where to start looking. Even though the wilderness areas do not require permits, it's still a good idea to stop off at the closest ranger station and let the Forest Service know where you will be hiking.

Equipment

Now comes the fun part, when you can run out and spend hundreds of dollars on all the latest high-tech backpacking equipment available in all the snazzy outdoor stores. Just kidding. While you *can* end up spending a near fortune on good equipment, there are ways to avoid depleting your pocketbook and still come up with the essentials for a safe, enjoyable backpack trip. John Muir, the father of much of our conservation ethic, experienced the wilderness with a blanket and a fishing rod before

Gore-tex and Holofil were household names. A positive wilderness experience is due largely to a state of mind, not the state of your bank account.

One way to become familiar with the proper and necessary equipment is to rent. Not only does this save you a huge capital outlay all at once, it allows you to try out several brands and models of equipment, such as internal or external frame packs and down or synthetic sleeping bags, before you buy. Then, as you decide on the advantages or disadvantages of each type of equipment, you can slowly invest in your own, piece by piece. Used equipment is sometimes available at outdoor stores, at equipment swaps, or advertised in the newspaper. Just be sure to check the items thoroughly, looking for holes, worn places, broken zippers, etc. Oftentimes, more experienced backpackers are looking to replace their older equipment with new, so ask friends to let you know if there's anything they want to sell.

BACKPACKS

This is your basic piece of equipment, your home away from home. It should be of good quality and chosen for fit and comfort. The two basic designs are external frame and internal frame. External frame packs should be constructed with welded or adjustable aluminum poles, a durable pack material with strong stitching and good quality zippers, and well padded shoulder and hip belts. Most external frame packs come with many small to medium size outside pockets which help organize your load and make gear accessible. There is a space at the bottom of the frame for your sleeping bag and extra room on top for additional gear. These packs are adequate for a week-long backpack trip and usually have extra bands or belts to hold excess equipment for longer hikes. I personally like the fit of these packs versus the internal frame packs—the weight rides high and rests primarily on your hips, and the external frame allows for ventilation next to your body, as opposed to the internal frame pack which tends to ride closer.

Internal frame packs are found in both a relatively small size for day trips or rock climbing trips, and huge, towering monsters intended for 10-day to two-week adventures. These frames are usually made of lightweight aluminum strips with pins, but should also be constructed of durable (nylon) material with well padded shoulder and hip straps. The larger packs are usually long and narrow with fewer outside pockets than on the external frame packs, but with more room inside for all your heavy gear. They also come with straps to tie on extra gear.

You should waterproof your pack before each trip (with spray silicon) and keep it as clean as possible for longer wear. Pack rain covers are sometimes available, and backpacking ponchos are designed to cover both you and your pack. Some reliable brand names include Kelty, Northface, Sierra Design, Jansport, and Mountainsmith, a relatively new manufacturer out of Colorado.

SLEEPING BAGS

Another essential backpack item, sleeping bags, come in all shapes, sizes, weights, and costs. The first choice you must make is between a synthetically filled (Holofil) or a down bag. Generally, down bags are more expensive but weigh less and have a lower temperature rating for colder camping. Synthetic bags have become very high-tech these days, however, and you can find bags rated to 0 degree Fahrenheit. I recommend investing in a down bag at a little extra cost because of the weight factor. A down bag rated for 20 degrees Fahrenheit, good for summer and fall camping, can weigh as little as two pounds. And one of the main goals in backpacking is to keep the weight down.

Both kinds of bags, synthetic and down, come in various shapes and sizes. The "mummy" bag is the most streamlined and generally the warmest. However, if you plan on camping only in warm weather, or if you're part of a couple and want bags that can zip together, you might consider purchasing a rectangular shaped bag for roominess and coolness.

For winter camping, most bags now come with attached hoods that can be pulled up over your head for complete protection. A new style of down bag comes with a Gore-tex finish and is supposed to be rain proof. I haven't tried it out yet, so you'll have to ask your trustworthy salesperson for verification.

GROUND PADS

I've known some backpackers who are quite happy sleeping in their bags directly on the ground (I'm sure John Muir was one of them), somehow conforming their bodies to all its bumps and depressions. But for those of us conditioned to the comforts of a padded mattress, some kind of ground pad is essential for both comfort and dryness. These can vary from a super-thin foam pad to the luxurious inflatable Thermarest pads now on the market. The price varies accordingly—five or six dollars for thinness and a certain amount of discomfort, to 40 or 50 dollars for thickness and a good night's sleep. Either way, you should pick a pad that is waterproof. On one trip, I remember my husband had what is called an "open cell" foam pad, which is generally thick and comfortable, but absorbs water. It was covered with a waterproof shell, however. My son, who can sleep anywhere on anything, had a "closed cell" foam pad, which is thin but waterproof. I had what is called an eggshell foam pad (like what is used in hospitals), which is nice, soft, and lightweight, but absorbs water. I woke up in the middle of a rainy night with my pad and bag soaked through from the wet floor of the tent. My husband and son were sound asleep in dry bags on pads that hadn't absorbed the water. I woke them up, of course, and we turned their pads sideways, below our shoulders and hips so three people could sleep on two pads. Fortunately, they love me and let me do this without too much complaining.

To assure both comfort and dryness, you can invest in a Thermarest pad, which inflates as you unroll it (you have to help it along by blowing it up to full capacity) and is covered with waterproof material. When you roll it back up, it conforms to a nice compact size for easy packing.

TENTS

Even though you may love sleeping out under the stars and find tents a nuisance, or claustrophobic, when there *are* no stars due to pouring rain, you better have a tent with a rainfly, or you'll be courting hypothermia.

Tents, like everything else, come in all shapes, sizes, and qualities. The first thing to decide is how large or small a tent you need. If you are single and usually go backpacking with friends who have all their own equipment, invest in a "two-person" tent. A "two-person" tent is in reality a comfortable one-person tent and a cramped two-person tent. This generally applies to all tent sizes: assume the tent holds one fewer persons that what is claimed, especially if you have any notion of keeping your pack in the tent with you. So if you are a family of four, you should have a five-or six-person tent, or several three-person tents to be comfortable. Everyone can carry a section of the tent to distribute the weight.

Quality is important. If you stay with reputable brands, you can be assured of well sewn seams and zippers, breathable material (to prevent condensation on the inside of the tent), collapsable

A four-person dome tent

lightweight poles, a well designed rainfly, cross ventilation, and screens on doors and windows.

Shapes of tents vary from domes and A-frames to long, low,

bivouacking tents. All the big manufacturers have variations of these standard shapes. A few criteria to help you decide what shape you want are: anticipated weather conditions, head room and maneuverability, degree of difficulty in setting up (and whether the tent is freestanding), and weight. If you are going to be carrying the tent all by yourself, you'll want to sacrifice roominess to keep the weight under seven pounds.

Before you venture out with a brand new tent, be sure you have sealed the seams (sealant is usually provided with new tents), and you know exactly how to assemble the tent—and what all the parts are for. You don't want to be figuring that out in the middle of a rainstorm or the middle of the night. Take along a plastic ground sheet to use as a moisture barrier and extra rope to tie the tent down (we once returned from a day's hike in Chaco Canyon to find our tent three campsites down the road after neglecting to tie it down in the perfectly still morning).

STOVES

Cooking over an open fire is my favorite way to prepare camp meals, but when backpacking, it's always a good idea to have a portable cook stove. If the weather is rainy and dry firewood hard to find, you'll appreciate a quick, hot meal cooked on a stove. Or if you've hiked all day and have to make a hurried camp before nightfall, it's much easier to cook a quick meal on a stove than prepare a fire and wait for hot coals to cook dinner. Some areas may have restrictions on campfires, or the area is so pristine you don't want to disturb any vegetation. Then a stove is indispensable.

There are many different brands and types of stoves that use different kinds of fuel: propane, butane, or white gas. Most of the brands you've heard of—Optimus, SVEA, Coleman, and MSR—use white gas, are light in weight, and easy to light The advantages in using white gas are its availability, dependability, high heat output, and responsiveness in cold weather. Several of the MSR and Coleman stoves burn both kerosene and white gas. Butane powered stoves are also easy to use but have a few disadvantages: higher cost, less availability, cold weather problems, a lower heat output, and disposable rather than reusable cartridges.

COOKING GEAR

In addition to your backpack stove, cooking items include a mess kit with plate, cup, cook pot, cup, knife, fork, and spoon.

These kits come in various combinations and sizes, and you should buy according to your needs. If you will usually be cooking for only one or two people, one mess kit with a small pot is all you need. If you have a family, you can buy extra pots and plates accordingly. Remember to include clean-up items such as dish soap (brought along in a screw-top plastic container) and a scrubber. And if you're a coffee addict, don't forget a small cone and filters for making fresh coffee.

SHOES

Proper hiking shoes are essential to a good backpack trip. If you have to contend with blisters and sore feet, you won't be much interested in beautiful scenery, getting to the top of the mountain, or exploring a new trail.

A good hiking boot should have a Vibram sole for traction, be high enough to support your ankle, sturdy enough for protection from rocks and rough trail conditions, waterproof, and most important, comfortable. The traditional heavy-duty, all leather boot still appeals to the serious backpacker carrying 60 to 80 pounds of weight on a week's trip in rough terrain. But these boots are quite heavy and very hard—sometimes impossible—to break in. I once owned a very expensive pair of Vasque boots that I *never* was able to break in, despite 11-mile hikes and everyday use. I'd inevitably come home with aching feet and at least one blister.

There are many other options for backpackers these days. Manufacturers now make all leather boots that provide reasonable support and durability without the excessive weight and stiffness of the older models. Popular now are the lighter weight boots of part leather and part Gore-tex or nylon, which provide some ankle support and durability but are geared more for a shorter, less rigorous hike. They do not hold up well in rough terrain, nor provide the kind of support and protection you need on long, difficult hikes.

Sneakers or jogging shoes are really not adequate for backpacking, but it's always a good idea to take along a lightweight pair to wear around camp or on day hikes from your base camp. Be sure to waterproof your leather boots with silicon or sno-seal before each trip.

SOCKS

No hiking boots will prevent blisters unless you wear the proper socks with them. The best combination is a lightweight liner sock next to the feet with a pair of wool socks or wool-synthetic combination sock as the outer layer. Research has shown that the synthetic materials such as polypropylene are better for liner socks than cotton, due to their ability to wick—repel—the perspiration from your feet. Some people also wear silk liners, as they do for cross-country skiing. Be sure to carry enough pairs of clean socks for each day of the trip. At night, put on the next day's pair of clean socks to keep your feet nice and toasty in your bag.

RAIN GEAR

Even in New Mexico, rain gear is a necessary backpack item. Your tent may keep you dry at night, but you can't very well wear it during the day. Most hikers opt for a rain poncho, which is easy to throw over both you and your pack and can double as a rain guard for your pack at night. Outdoor stores carry special backpack ponchos that have extra length to cover your pack, but regular, inexpensive ponchos are also adequate. Instead of a poncho you can invest (and it's a big investment) in a Gore-tex rain jacket and pants outfit, which is about the only thing that will *really* keep you dry in a drenching rainstorm. Without Gore-tex you might want to consider just stopping and sitting out the storm under a rain tarp.

A few tips before heading out on what is obviously going to be a rainy hike: 1) wear shorts if the weather is warm enough, as skin dries faster than the bottom part of your pants, which will invariably get wet; 2) make sure your boots are waterproofed; and 3) pack the items you'll need quick access to, like water, food, and an extra sweater, in easily reached pockets of your pack.

EXTRA CLOTHING

The type and amount of extra clothing you have to pack for a trip depends, of course, on the season and altitude of your hike. Generally, you should carry a minimum amount of lightweight clothes that will provide adequate warmth for cold weather and comfort for hot weather. Your list should include a pair of shorts, a pair of long pants or sweatpants, clean underwear and socks for each day, a sweatshirt or wool shirt, several t-shirts; a heavy parka or vest and long underwear for really cold weather, a hat for sun protection, a bandana, and an extra pair of lightweight shoes.

WATER CONTAINERS AND PURIFIERS

The amount of water you must carry from home depends upon the availability of water on the trail. A quart of water weighs two pounds and can be your heaviest backpack item if you have to carry all your supply. Having to carry more than a gallon of water at a time may well cause you to change your choice of trail. Lightweight, screw-top plastic water bottles in quart or quart and a half sizes are available in all outdoor stores. You can also purchase collapsible gallon containers, but these are really too big and bulky to carry up the trail (but do come in handy for storing water at camp). The smaller size jugs can fit into outside pockets of your pack for easy access. In the summer you need at least one quart (preferably two) of water per day for drinking, plus another quart or two for camp.

The Forest Service recommends that all stream, lake, and spring water be purified before use. The only exception I make is for spring water that is piped directly from underground with no possibility of contamination. Most contaminants are the result of small rodents in the water source. Four purification methods are available: mechanical filtration, iodine, chlorine, and boiling.

Boiling is the surest method to kill the three basic types of contaminants: bacteria, viruses, and amoebic cysts. A minute boil (three or four minutes at higher elevations) will kill Giardia lamblia, the most pernicious of the intestinal parasites, and 10 minutes kills other bacteria and viruses. The biggest drawback to boiling is the time it takes to boil and cool your water supply. At camp it's a good idea to boil your daily water supply the night before, so it has time to cool in the nighttime air. Boiling also consumes more fuel, either your packed-in source or wood for your campfire.

Mechanical filtration, with pumps that cost anywhere from $25 to $200, are reputed to prevent Giardia, as the parasite cannot get through the filter, but do allow the smaller viruses through. Contracting a virus like hepatitis is unlikely, but if you camp in an area where there is a possibility of this particular virus, a filter is not adequate. A recent study has caused some dispute as to the reliability of the filter even against Giardia (there is evidence the cysts can survive in the filter), and researchers recommend that you buy the more expensive filters that have pre-filters or filters that can be cleaned after each use. Some filters are now made with a silver lining that eliminates bacterial growth in the filter. If you do use the less expensive mechanical filters, be sure to replace the filter as soon as it begins to clog and look dirty (the filters come with recommended usage time as well as tips on storage and cleaning). With any mechanical filter, it's a good idea to collect your water in a pot and let it stand for the debris to settle before filtering.

While chlorine kills bacteria and viruses, it has been determined that Giardia has a resistance to it. Consequently, the chlorine tablets sold in outdoor stores labeled Halozone are not adequate to decontaminate the water. Iodine is the more effective chemical and is sold in the stores as Potable Agua (hyperiodide), which comes in tablets, or iodine crystals, which must be measured. Add one tablet to a quart of water (two if the water is especially dirty) with the lid securely fastened, for at least 20 minutes. Both chlorine and iodine have an unpleasant taste, which makes them less desirable methods of purification. There is a new product marketed by a firm in Santa Fe that uses chlorine as a purifier (they claim it *does* kill Giardia) and hydrogen peroxide to counteract the taste of the chlorine.

Miscellaneous Equipment

SUNSCREEN

Being out for days at a time, especially at high altitudes, calls for plenty of sunscreen on your face (and on your ears and head if you lack much hair). Wear sunscreen even if you wear a hat, as nothing protects as well. And remember to reapply several times during the day.

SUNGLASSES

It's a good idea to take along sunglasses, even if you normally don't wear them, as exposure to the sun over a long period of time can strain your eyes.

INSECT REPELLENT

I've been on trips that were battles with the bugs—mostly mosquitoes—which I lost without repellent. If you plan on camping near water, you're going to be joined by mosquitoes, which can make an otherwise pleasurable situation miserable. Commercial repellents are usually repellent to you as well (they stink), so you may want to try some herbal repellents or rub garlic on your skin, which has proven to be effective and tasty.

FLASHLIGHT
Outdoor stores now carry small, compact flashlights suitable for backpacking. Be sure to carry extra batteries on a lengthy trip.

COMPASS
You may find that you never use a compass, but it may prove indispensable if you become disoriented or lost.

PLASTIC GARBAGE BAGS
These can be used for both garbage—your own and any you find on the trail—as well as rain gear for your pack.

POCKET KNIFE
A good Swiss army knife will serve as your carving knife, can opener, scissors, file, and toothpick.

MATCHES
It's a good idea to carry both kitchen matches and book matches in a plastic, waterproof container or ziplock bag. A pocket lighter also comes in handy for hard-to-start fires.

FIRST AID KIT
With careful planning it's rare that a hiker risks serious injury on a backpack trip, but there's always the possibility that minor cuts, blisters, or bruises can occur. It's a good idea to carry a small first aid kit to attend these injuries.

Moleskin (or second skin) is a must. Even the most broken-in boots in the world can raise a blister on a long, arduous hike, so it's wise to prevent possible blisters by applying moleskin to sensitive areas—across the back of the heel or along the side of the big toe. Or you can wait until a spot becomes slightly irritated and then apply the moleskin. Just don't wait until the blister appears, because then even moleskin won't protect you from the pain.

Include a sampling of bandaids in your kit. Take along a dozen or so regular size bandaids, a small package of sterile pads with adhesive tape, and an ace bandage. The latter is particularly important if you have weak knees or ankles and need to wrap either for extra protection.

I always include some kind of pain pill in anticipation of headaches (which can easily occur on long, hot hikes) or to ease the pain of minor injuries. If you are on medication for some ailment, be sure and take it along, too. Other first aid items include antibiotic ointment, a small pair of scissors, tweezers, and Lomotil tablets.

MAPS

There are many kinds of maps available through the Forest Service and outdoor stores. Topographic maps, with elevation lines, are the most detailed, although many of the U.S. Geological Survey maps need to be updated to show the location of new trails or relocated trails. It's a good idea to use these maps in conjunction with a Forest Service map. Wilderness area maps are available for all the New Mexico wildernesses, and many of them have been recently updated. Most of these maps have elevation lines and are quite detailed. You can obtain them from the closest Forest Service ranger station or appropriate supervisor's office, along with district maps, which provide a good overview of the area. Carry your maps in an outside pocket of your pack in a waterproof bag, so you can easily—and often—stop and check your location. The maps that accompany the trail descriptions in this book show the general location of the hike—trailheads, trail junctions, and major landmarks along the route. You should purchase a more detailed map of each wilderness area to supplement this book.

PERSONAL ITEMS

A minimum of personal items will keep you decently clean (you never know who you might meet on the trail) without adding much weight to your pack. Include the following items: bar soap, small towel, toilet paper, toothbrush and toothpaste, hairbrush, and lip balm.

DAYPACK

Many backpack trips mean hiking to a destination, making a base camp, then taking day trips from there. Take along a relatively small daypack (fanny packs are good for this) to carry essential day trip items such as water, lunch, and rain gear. You can easily hang an empty daypack on the outside of your backpack.

Food

Food choices are largely personal, of course, but there are ways to plan menus that make eating on the trail like eating at home (almost) rather than an exercise in depravation. Long backpack trips do require some spartan meals, but on most two-to seven-day hikes you can combine fresh food with packaged, coming up with some nutritious and tasty meals. When planning your trip, write out a menu for each day, then add an extra day's food for an emergency. Several recipes from friends are included here after the following list of suggested food items.

Main course: freeze dried or dehydrated food packs, quick rice, noodles, ramen soups, instant soup mixes, vegetables for stir fry, small frozen shrimp for stir fry, instant mashed potatoes, couscous, bulgur.

Lunch: cheese and crackers, vegetable sticks, dried fruit, rice cakes with peanut butter and honey, instant soup, canned sardines or smoked oysters.

Breakfast: eggs, potatoes, English muffins, pancakes, granola, dried fruit.

Condiments: salt and pepper, garlic, cooking oil, onion, chile powder, soy sauce, sesame oil, curry powder.

Miscellaneous: trail mix, pemican bars, granola bars, pretzels or tortilla chips, salsa.

Drinks: Gatorade, juice, lemonade mix, cocoa mix, coffee, tea, powdered milk.

For summer hikes you can premix some juice and freeze it in your plastic water bottles (do the same with your water) for cold drinks on the first several days' hikes.

Jinkle Seagrave's Chicken Dumplings

2 cups dried chicken or one 8 oz. can
$1/4$ cup dried carrots
$1/4$ cup dried peas
$1/4$ cup dried mushrooms
2 tbsp. onion
1 tsp. garlic powder or 2 cloves
1 tbsp. bouillon
$1/2$ tsp. each parsley, sage, thyme

$^1/_4$ cup flour
$^1/_2$ cup dried milk

Add water to a baggy of your dried vegetables two hours before cooking. In a fairly deep stew pot bring water and the vegetables to a simmer, then add the chicken and bouillon. Stir in the spices, flour, milk, and simmer for 15 minutes.

Dumplings:
1 cup Bisquick
$^1/_2$ cup Parmesan cheese (optional)
1 tbsp. parsley

Add enough water to make a soft dough, about $^1/_3$ cup. Drop balls of dough onto simmering stew, cover, and cook for about 15 minutes or until dough is cooked through. Serves 3-4.

Stephen Maurer's Chile con Carne

2 lbs. lean pork, beef or game
6 tbsp. red chile powder
1 tbsp. flour
4 cloves garlic, crushed
1 tsp. oregano
4 tbsp. oil
salt

Trim fat from meat and cut into $^1/_2$ inch cubes. Fry in hot oil, stirring frequently, until the liquid that is released cooks away and meat begins to brown. Sprinkle with flour and brown slightly. Add chile powder, half of the crushed garlic, and enough water to stir, not too thick. Add salt, oregano, turn heat down, and simmer until meat is done and the liquid is the consistency of a thick sauce (approximately $1^1/_2$ to 2 hours). Add remaining garlic and cook for 5 minutes longer. Spread out on cookie sheets or on aluminum foil and dry in the sun, in a 140 degree oven, or in a dehydrator.
Yields about 8-10 oz.

To reconstitute:
Put desired portion in a container with a tight fitting top, 12-24 hours before cooking (wide mouth plastic containers with screw-top lids work very well and weigh little). Pour on enough water to cover by 1/2 inch. Stow away in your pack. By mealtime most of the liquid will have been absorbed; pour into a pan and heat. Serve with refried beans and tortillas.

Refried beans

Cook pinto beans in pressure cooker or crock pot until nice and tender. Season to taste with salt, pepper, and garlic. Drain liquid off beans, mash, and dry in the same manner as described above.

To reconstitute
Add water to the beans and let stand for a few minutes. Stir well and fry in a little oil.

Nancy and Marcos' Rice Casserole

1 package Spanish rice mix (in health food stores)
1 package sun-dried tomatoes
1/2 cup cheddar cheese

Cook the rice according to the instructions, in a large pot with lid. Add the sun-dried tomatoes after most of the liquid is gone, then cover with sliced or grated cheese and let sit until cheese melts.

CAMP ETIQUETTE

Most of the described hikes are in wilderness areas where the stated creed is "man is a visitor only." And the kind of visitor that implies is one who leaves little or no trace that he or she has been one. While the "wildman" of the Pecos carries only his knife and blanket and spends months at a time communing with the bears, the rest of us, with our high-tech equipment, must try to commune with nature in as benign a fashion as possible. We are indeed visitors only; we'd never make it through a summer on berries or a winter on bark. So it's our responsibility to leave things as we found them, as close to a "natural" state as we'll ever know. Our New Mexico wilderness areas may not be anything like what the grizzly and wolf inhabited 200 years ago, but they are now ours to protect and preserve.

Campsites

Pick a campsite where the terrain can withstand a tent and camping activity without showing too much wear and tear. In other words, don't pitch your tent on that nice tall grass in the middle of an alpine meadow, but put it over on the sandy edge of the forest or on the pine needles under a spruce tree. Pick a site with good drainage (it's sometimes hard to tell until you wake up in the middle of the night with a soaking wet tent floor), so you don't have to dig a trench around your tent. Don't put nails in trees to secure the tent; use stakes in the ground or ropes tied around trees. When you break camp, go over the area thoroughly for garbage, and cover up the evidence of your presence as best you can.

Campfires

If you find the remains of previous fires, it's best to use the same site for your fire. Although campers are supposed to scatter the stones from their fire rings and leave the site looking as natural as possible, you can almost always find previous campfire remains. Make sure the area is open (not under a tree) and cleared of vegetation, and ring your fire pit with rocks. Keep the fire small so as to disturb as little ground as possible and to use as little wood as possible. A campfire need not be large to cook with or provide warmth. Gather only dead and down wood for your fire; unless you have carried in a hatchet or axe, you'll be able to carry only small branches and twigs.

When breaking camp put out your fire with dirt and water (if available), and bury the remains. Unless the campfire is obviously

Getting a pyramid-shaped fire started in a well cleared area

the area as natural looking as possible. Oftentimes, fire restrictions are in effect due to extreme weather conditions, so always check with the local Forest Service ranger station before your trip. Some areas prohibit campfires entirely.

Washing

Steams and lakes are for collecting water, not to be used as washtubs. When washing dishes—or yourself—wash and rinse, with soap or biodegradable detergent, well back from the shores of the water source. Never throw your waste-water back into the stream or lake. We have enough polluted water sources where we live without polluting those where we visit. And never throw your fish heads or entrails back into the water—please!

Sanitation

If you are camping by yourself or with a small group, it's not necessary to dig group latrines for a sanitary campsite. Go well away from camp or any water source and dig individual holes in the topsoil (a couple of inches deep) for better decomposition. Bury your waste but burn your toilet paper.

Garbage

Forest Service policy prohibits burying any of your garbage, organic or inorganic. Pack in a garbage bag to carry out all the trash you can't burn. Items like tin foil, cans, bottles, plastic, orange and banana peels cannot be burned (not that you should be carrying in cans and bottles in the first place). Double check your campsite for small litter when you leave, and be a sport—carry out anyone else's garbage from the campsite or trail as well.

Trails

Many trails in our New Mexico wilderness areas are in various states of disrepair, due to heavy human use, pack animal use, and lack of maintenance by the Forest Service (due to lack of funding and misplaced priorities in spending). Oftentimes, new routes on trails are blazed within a matter of days as detours around fallen logs, washouts, etc., revealing how fragile the landscape is. Try to avoid blazing these new routes yourself or cutting switchbacks and causing erosion. Most forest trails have been laid out to prevent erosion or other kinds of damage to the terrain, so stick to the given trail whenever possible. This may be next to impossible on a rainy day behind a pack train, but try not to leave a new trail

Following a wide path through the Pecos

for others to follow. When you do come across obstacles on the trail, move them if you can, or notify the ranger station when you get back to civilization. Please don't leave cairns (rocks piled up as markers) or mark up trees as trail indicators. Again, notify the Forest Service about trail signs that are down or vandalized. Maybe if enough of us complain, more money will be spent on wilderness maintenance than paving roads.

Pets

I have taken my dogs into the wilderness with me, especially on day hikes in the Sandia Mountains behind my house, but I understand the rationale for not doing so. Dogs can be very disruptive and annoying to other campers and can destroy any chance of seeing wildlife. If you do take your dog with you, keep it on a leash, especially at night (or in the tent, if it's a three dog night), or under verbal command at all times.

SAFETY

Getting Lost

As I said before, always let someone know where you are hiking and when you plan to return. That way, if you *do* get lost, a search party will know in what vicinity to look for you.

If for some reason you lose the trail, stop immediately and regroup. Try to recall how far back you may have taken a wrong turn or lost the trail, then try and backtrack to that point. You may be able to retrace your footprints in soft or wet dirt. A compass will keep you pointed in the right direction as indicated by your map. Read your map carefully to identify any landmarks that might help you find where you are in relation to the trail. You need not panic if you cannot find the trail within a reasonable length of time—you have your sustenance and home on your back. Take off your pack, relax, and start blowing your whistle to make contact with other hikers. You will eventually be found by hikers or search and rescue personnel. All search efforts are coordinated through the State Police with local search and rescue groups, who are well trained. I found out how well trained they are when I hiked—inadvertently—with 40 of them in the Pecos. From Las Vegas and St. John's College, they entered the wilderness from both sides and quickly surrounded us with their litters and walkie-talkies, spoiling any solitude we sought on that hike but reassuring us that they would always find us, wherever we were. That particular day we wished we weren't in the Pecos.

Hypothermia

Hypothermia is the lowering of the inner body core temperature due to cold, windy, or wet conditions. Symptoms include shivering, fatigue, disorientation, numbness, slow pulse, blue lips, and slurred speech. If not treated immediately, the body temperature can descend irreversibly. Treatment includes taking the victim to shelter, removing wet clothing and warming with a fire, sleeping bag, body heat or hot bath.

Camping at high altitudes where extreme weather conditions occur necessitates that preventive measures be taken. Know your hiking limitations (and those of your companions), and don't attempt trips that may be too taxing for your endurance level. If you are attempting an ascent into alpine country and a storm is brewing, consider abandoning your goal and staying at a lower elevation to avoid extreme cold and moisture. If you are caught in a rainstorm—or snowstorm—-stop and put on your rain gear or make an early camp, so you can shelter in your tent.

Altitude Sickness

This usually occurs above 7,000 feet and is characterized by dizziness, headache, shortness of breath, lack of energy, and nausea. If you begin to feel any of these symptoms, stop, rest, drink fluids, eat some high-energy food, and return to lower elevations. The best prevention is to be sure you're in good physical condition and somewhat acclimated to the climate and altitude where you will be hiking. That's not always possible when you're climbing Wheeler Peak or some other 13,000-foot peak—and you'll find that you'll almost always experience a certain amount of shortness of breath and light-headedness—but you can accomplish the hike if you prepare adequately.

Physical Conditioning

If you are in reasonable physical shape, a backpack trip is not a beast of burden marathon but a wonderful way to see the backcountry you cannot reach on day hikes. The best preparation for a good trip is year-round physical activity, such as swimming, cross-country skiing, bike riding, jogging, etc., but as summer approaches and you anticipate a long backpack trip, you might want to concentrate on some regular exercise. At least 20 to 30 minutes of exercise three to five times a week to get your cardio-vascular system going should be undertaken several months before your trip. If you like to avoid spas and exercise classes where exercise for beauty sometimes overshadows exercise for health, achieve your conditioning by playing basketball or rac-quetball, jogging around the park a few times, or practicing with your kid's soccer team. If you can stay with them up and down the field, you can make it to the top of Wheeler.

Information

Listed below are the names, address, and telephone numbers of the various ranger districts that service the three wilderness areas. You can contact any of these offices for more information, or to let them know your backpacking itinerary.

CARSON NATIONAL FOREST
Supervisor's Office
208 Cruz Alta Road
Taos, NM 87571
(505) 758-6292

Camino Real Ranger District
P.O. Box 348
Peñasco, NM 87553
(505) 587-2255

Taos Ranger District
P.O. Box 558
Taos, NM 87571
(505) 758-2911

SANTA FE NATIONAL FOREST
Supervisor's Office
1220 St. Francis Drive
Santa Fe, NM 87504
(505) 988-6940

Pecos Ranger District
P.O. Box 429
Pecos, NM 87552
(505) 757-6121

Española Ranger District
P.O. Box R
Española, NM 87532
(505) 753-7331

Las Vegas Ranger District
1926 N. Seventh Street
Las Vegas, NM 87701
(505) 425-3534

Coyote Ranger District
Coyote, NM 87012
(505) 638-5547

Cuba Ranger District
Cuba, NM 87013
(505) 289-3265

BACKPACKING WITH CHILDREN

While for some of you, backpacking with your children might defeat the purpose of your trip—to get away to the wilderness where you can enjoy solitude and repose—others may have no choice or may want to be a family together in the wilderness. My older son Jakob has been backpacking with us since he was four, and my younger son Max just went on his first backpack trip at the tender age of 22 months (he was backpacked, along with everything else). Here are some tips on how to make an excursion with your children as pleasant—and relaxing—as possible.

Planning

If you plan on taking a child who will obviously be unable to do much, if any, hiking, you will need several essential items: 1) a child backpack carrier that will enable you to also pack in some items besides the baby and 2) some helpful friends willing to go backpacking with you and share the load (just assure them they won't have to sleep with the baby, too). Most mountaineering stores carry child backpacks that are well-built and designed to fit like a regular backpack, meaning they rest the load on your hips, not your shoulders. They have pockets and straps for carrying some of your gear,too, although by the time you pack the baby, you'll probably not want to carry much more than some clothes, a sleeping bag, and diapers (more on that later). Unfortunately, the packs are usually quite expensive, so if you can find a used one or borrow one from a friend, it will save investing in something you'll use for only a few years. Remember, too, that a 25-pound baby is not exactly comparable to a 25-pound load of camping gear that doesn't wiggle around, list from side to side, and scream in your ear occasionally. My husband carried our son Max on his first trip in a regular Gerry carrier (with extra padding), with a sleeping bag and day pack of diapers and bottles strapped on, and while he was a good sport about it, I'm sure his shoulders were screaming as loud as our son (actually, the baby loved being carried about and did very little complaining).

If your child is of hiking age, which is usually five or older, depending upon the child, you can buy a child's backpack, so he or she can carry most of their own gear. Jakob usually carries all

Kids playing at the lakeshore

his clothes, his sleeping bag and ground pad, a quart of water, his fishing pole and tackle, and some trail snacks. That doesn't mean that there won't be some complaining about how heavy their packs are, but when they graduate to a full-fledged pack, they'll realize how easy we were on them back in the good old days. If you can, bring along one of your kid's friends who has his or her own gear, as there's likely to be a lot less complaining when there's a certain amount of distraction and competition among friends as to who's the better hiker, who's carrying the heaviest pack, etc.

Be realistic about where you want to go—how far it is, how difficult the terrain will be, if there is an adequate water supply, and if it is too high in elevation to safely take a baby. Even if you have friends helping with the load, you are not going to be able to walk as many miles as you normally do on a backpack trip. Even if you can take it, your child or baby probably can't. Most kids will tolerate only three or four hours per day on the trail or in a back carrier. They need to be able to run around and explore as well as watch the scenery from their mom's or dad's shoulders.

If the terrain is particularly taxing, no one will enjoy the trip. We took Max on his first trip to San Pedro Parks, where the trails are easy to hike and provide lots of open, grassy meadows for him to run around and play in. You don't want to have to worry about precarious climbs with a baby on your back or no place to put the baby down to rest without constant supervision.

San Pedro Parks was also a good place to take a baby because of an abundance of water. Not only do you need a good water source if you plan on using cloth diapers (more on that below), but a baby always gets dirtier faster and more often than anyone else and seems to require constant washings (but don't overdo it—one is supposed to be somewhat dirty while camping, especially kids).

I think it's best to take your kids or baby on a trip that stays at or below the 10,000 foot elevation. Above that you are taking risks that might make the situation unsafe: nighttime temperatures can drop quite low, and unpredictable weather can turn a pleasant experience into a nightmare. We once took Jakob, when he was nine years old, on an overnight trip in the Pecos Wilderness to Spirit and Katherine Lakes. The first night was fine, at Spirit. The weather was mild, and even though it was August, there was no rain. We decided to walk out via Lake Katherine, which would make the day's hike more than 10 miles, but our son is an experienced, strong hiker, and we knew he could do it. Unfortunately, when we reached Katherine, which sits in a glacial bowl at 12,000 feet, a lightening and hail storm swept in, and our trip became miserable. Jakob was frightened of the lightning (we were too, but tried to hide it), and despite our rain gear and wool sweaters, we all got quite cold (there were several inches of standing water on the trail, and our feet were soaked). It rained the whole way back to the Santa Fe Ski Basin, and while Jakob was a real trooper and quit complaining once it became apparent it wasn't going to help the situation to whine, he had a lousy time, and we felt badly for him. Fortunately, we would never have considered taking the baby on such a trip, as we wouldn't have been able to keep him warm or carry him on such an arduous hike.

Plan your trip so that you can hike into a specific destination, establish a base camp, and take day hikes from there. That way you don't have to carry the baby and all your gear every day, and there is more time for the kids to play and you to relax—or spend one whole day at camp, just lying around, fishing, cooking, and playing. After all, backpacking is supposed to be fun, not a marathon adventure.

Clothing

You always have to pack more for a kid than you do for yourself, especially if you have a baby still in diapers. I plan on two outfits per day: shorts and a t-shirt for warm, daytime temperatures; pants (or overalls) and a long-sleeved top for the evening or if the weather turns colder during the day. I usually take a heavy pair of pajamas (with feet) for each night, just in case they get wet and it's impossible to dry them during the day. A "Baby Bag"—a quilted sleeping bag equipped with feet—is even better for use on cold nights around the campfire and as a sleeping bag. Take clean socks for each day, an extra pair of woolen socks in case it gets cold, several sweatshirts or sweaters, and an extra pair of shoes. Just as you do for yourself, pack a sun hat, wool hat, and mittens. Unless I will be camping in a low, warm area, I always take the baby's parka, too. Always include rain gear that will fit over the carrier, or an extra poncho or rain jacket just for the baby. Children's ponchos are available in most outdoor stores. For older chilren, take along plenty of plastic bags that fit over their boots for hiking in the rain.

Diapers

The big question is, of course, do you take plastic or cloth diapers (unless you are a purist and absolutely refuse to consider plastic). For a trip of three days or less, and if you have some friends who are helping to carry the load, the easiest way to go is plastic diapers. They usually don't have to be changed as often as cloth ones, so you can get by with fewer, and they can be carried out in plastic bags. I always take along some cloth diapers, too, just in case I miscalculate the number of plastic diapers I'll need. They make good nose wipes anyway.

If the trip is longer than three days, I think the burden (and waste) of plastic diapers becomes too much. What you must consider for a longer trip is having an adequate water supply to be able to wash cloth diapers for reuse (and hopefully plenty of sun to dry them as well). Pack enough diapers for several day's use, so you have a day's worth of diapers to spare if it's rainy, and the diapers take a long time to dry. If you keep the diapers washed, you won't have to carry around the extra weight of wet diapers.

Take plenty of plastic bags for between washings—and plenty of plastic or nylon pants.

Bottles

If your baby still takes a bottle, plan on introducing a little powdered milk (mixed half and half with whole milk) in his or her bottle a few days before the trip, so it's not such a shock when there's no more fresh milk after the second or third day. You can provide fresh milk until then if you freeze two or three bottles of milk before you leave. In the mountains the weather is usually cool enough to keep the bottles from spoiling for at least several days. You can do the same with juice—freeze before leaving and keep in the shade during the day.

Take plenty of powdered instant milk to supplement your fresh supply. You can begin mixing the powdered with the fresh before it runs out, to make it more palatable, but eventually you'll have to rely completely on the instant. I was sure my son would have a fit the first time he tasted it in his bottle, but he drank it right down without a complaint. You must be extra cautious that your water supply is uncontaminated, of course. I recommend boiling any water you will be using to make the instant milk.

Food

Take lots of nonperishable snacks the kids particularly like and can carry, such as trail mix, dried fruit, jerky, sucking candies, and granola bars. Otherwise just assume your kids will eat what you eat, to keep food preparation as simple as possible.

Sleeping Bags

We always let the kids have the warmest down bags, in case of extrememly cold weather. And we always bring the baby's own sleeping bag (or Baby Bag) and ground pad, as it's impossible to keep a baby covered with your open bag or attempt to share a bag with a baby. Don't plan on many romantic moments, because it's best to keep the baby between you in the tent, so you can both keep an eye on him or her. Max constantly attempts to squirm out of his bag, so it takes a lot of rearranging throughout the night to keep him warm. Jakob, on the other hand, can sleep anywhere, through anything, and never wake up.

Max and Mark out in the wildernesss

MAP LEGEND

- - - - - - -	Trail
...■..■..■ ..	Intermittant Stream
== =======	Dirt road
▬▬▬▬▬	Paved road
■ ·■·■·■·■	Wilderness boundary
⚑	Picnic ground or campground
△	Peak
∫	Spring

Section II. Wheeler Peak Wilderness

Mabel Dodge Lujan always called Wheeler Peak the "sacred mountain" and gave up a comfortable New York life to live in its power zone. Sacred to the Taos Indians, guardian of the Hispanic settlements at its foot, and destination of the Anglo miner, trapper, and forester, Wheeler has always played a powerful role in the lives of northern New Mexicans. Its blue-green summer shadow and white-capped winter silhouette create a consciousness that is not only the mountain's own, but is embedded in the lives of those in its presence.

At 13,161 feet, the peak is the high point of the crescent shaped Sangre de Cristo range encircling the Taos Valley. Wheeler is only one of several peaks of slightly less elevation that make the Wheeler Peak Wilderness the most rugged and wild area of New Mexico. While only 20,727 acres large, the wilderness contains a wide diversity of terrain, including alpine tundra vegetation, glacial cirques filled with deep blue lakes, dense stands of spruce-fir forests, and meadows of wildflowers and native grasses. Animals include the high altitude marmot and pika, the black bear, Rocky Mountain bighorn sheep, mountain lion, numerous small mammals, and hundreds of species of birds The gray jay, colloquially referred to as "camp robber," loves to see folks headed up the mountain and will tag along for any treats that might come its way. We've had them sitting on our hands eating stoneground wheat crackers at Bull-of-the-Woods. Unusual tundra flowers grow in the above timberline meadows, and the Colorado state flower, the blue columbine, proliferates throughout the Canadian and Hudsonian zones.

Although the wilderness area is rather small, the surrounding country provides additional backcountry opportunities. Included in the RARE II study area for possible wilderness designation is the Hondo-Columbine area north of Wheeler Peak, accessed by trails from all directions. Evidence of the intense mining activity of the late 19th and early 20th centuries is everywhere, from Twining to Gold Hill to Pioneer Lake. Columbine-Twining National Recreation Trail leads from Columbine Campground near Red River to the Taos Ski Valley, offering terrain and views as diverse and spectacular as any within the wilderness.

Because of the high elevations of the mountain peaks and the danger of summer lightning storms, the hiking season in this area is somewhat limited. Mabel Dodge describes in her book her impatience waiting through that first Taos winter for the snow to melt off the peaks and the spring muds to dry up, so she could get out and experience "the mountain." Then in July, on a horseback trip to Blue Lake, sacred site of Taos Pueblo, her party got drenched by the summer showers that come every afternoon to chase away the sun. In the past few years several people have actually been struck by lightning attempting to climb Wheeler Peak, so make your ascent in June, before the rains come (if the snow has melted by then) or in the fall before the new snow.

Access to the Wheeler Peak Wilderness is from the west through the Taos Ski Valley or from the northeast via the town of Red River.

Feeding a gray jay in the Wheeler Peak Wilderness

Red River Access

Access to the Wheeler Peak Wilderness Area from the east is via Red River, a resort town east of Taos that looks like anywhere but New Mexico with its cowboy-front buildings and satellite dish cabins. But once you've left town and are headed up the East, Middle, or West Fork Trails toward Wheeler Peak, you're back in the bosom of the New Mexico high country. East and Middle Fork Trails can be hiked as a loop trail and as access to Wheeler Peak; West Fork Trail connects with Bull-of-the-Woods Trail and the west side Taos Ski Valley trails.

EAST FORK RIVER TRAIL #56:
6.5 miles   Moderate   Elevation: 9,600-11,500 feet

From the junction of SH 38 and 150 south of Red River it's 6 miles via 150 to a sign on Forest Road 58 which says: East Fork 2, West Fork, Middle Fork. Follow the East Fork arrow to the left to FR 58A, which bears south through a summer home area (be sure to close the gates after you) to the wilderness gateway sign. Park here by the river and hike the four-wheel drive road which leads .5 mile to the Ditch Cabin site where the road narrows to a trail. This area was extensively mined in the latter part of the 19th century, and portions of the Elizabeth Ditch are visible alongside many of the Red River trails. A log bridge crosses over a creek to a sign which reads: East Fork Trail #56, Sawmill Park 2, Horseshoe Lake 6. The trail travels south on the east side of the East Fork in a gentle ascent for 1 mile to the junction with Sawmill Park Trail #55; Sawmill Park is to the east 1 mile and the Taos Cone 8 miles. East Fork River Trail continues south along the river (which is quite a ways down in the canyon) through lush vegetation of camas, woodnymph, geranium, bluebell, larkspur, and shooting star.

At about 3 miles, the trail crosses a creek on a wooden bridge and enters the wilderness. Old Lost Lake Trail—no longer in use—is found to the west, while East Fork Trail continues southwest. The path is quite wet here as it climbs out of the canyon toward the west now, across another stream and past a marshy meadow on the right.

Up on the ridge the trail crosses the talus slopes where the marmots sit on the rocks sunning themselves in the cold, clear air.

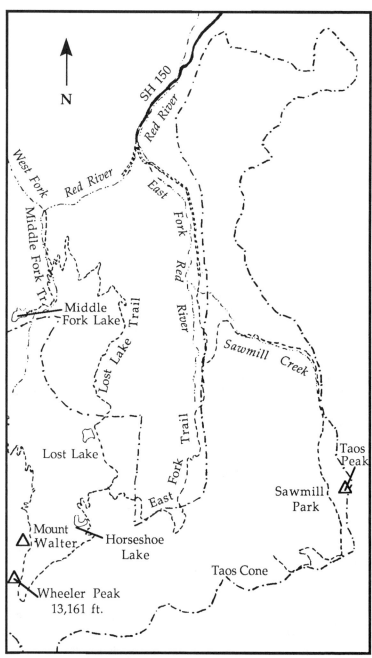

EAST FORK FORK TRAIL #56

If you approach quietly, they will let you get quite close. The trail crests to a view of the high peaks north and west. Climbing northwest now, the trail crosses another stream, then crosses the waterfall bridge. While these are good water sources, and there are several campsites here, they don't provide much privacy. Just past the bridge is the junction of the trail to Horseshoe Lake, heading 1 mile west, the main route to Wheeler Peak, which is a 3-mile climb from the lake. East Fork Trail continues another mile north to Lost Lake. Just below the lake, signs indicate no camping within a certain radius of the lake to protect the fragile shoreline. The lake itself sits in a beautiful glacial bowl deepened by the damming of the river to supply the Elizabethtown Ditch, a 42-mile canal built in 1868 to provide water to the mining operations in Elizabethtown, now a ghost town near present day Eagle Nest. The towering Wheeler Peak is its backdrop. Lost Lake Trail leads north from the lake and ties in with Middle Fork Lake Trail back down to FR 58.

WHEELER PEAK VIA HORSESHOE LAKE TRAIL:
3 miles   Difficult   Elevation: 12,000-13,161 feet

To climb Wheeler Peak from the Red River side, it's best to make a base camp at Lost Lake or Horseshoe Lake, so you can reach the top of the mountain by early day and avoid the ubiquitous rain and lightning storms of summer afternoons. Ideally, if you can climb Wheeler in late June after the snow melts, or in the fall before the snow flies, you're most likely to avoid the dangerous weather. Horseshoe Lake Trail intersects East Fork Trail a mile before you get to Lost Lake and climbs almost another mile to the damned, horseshoe-shaped lake below Wheeler. A sign at the peak access trail indicates it's 3 miles to the top.

The trail, in a steady climb, ascends the ridge south of the lake toward Old Mike Peak. You then climb to the ridge just south of Wheeler Peak, and at a little over 1 mile, you reach the trail following the Wheeler ridge, Crest Trail #90. Turn to the right (left goes to Simpson and Old Mike Peak) to ascend to the final turn at another .5 miles. The trail along the ridge passes the peak on the east side, and the trail to the top of Wheeler doubles back off this trail. Once you've collapsed on the top of New Mexico, caught your breath, and marveled at the unparalleled view over both valleys, you can continue north on Trail #90 another .5 miles to

Old Man's Beard hanging from a high-country fir

Mount Walter, then past the west side ascent trail from Williams Lake, and on to Bull-of-the-Woods Trail.

MIDDLE FORK LAKE TRAIL #140:
2 miles   Moderate   Elevation: 9,600-10,800 feet

This hike is outside the wilderness boundary but connects with Lost Lake Trail, which enters the wilderness beyond the junction of the two trails. To reach the trailhead, take SH 150 out of Red River 6 miles to the end of the pavement. A directional sign points west on FR 58 to the Middle Fork-West Fork trailhead

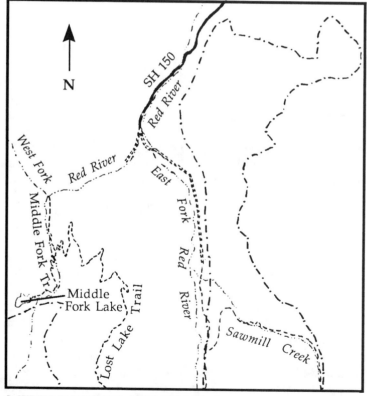

MIDDLE FORK LAKE TRAIL #140

parking area, about 1 mile beyond the pavement.

From the parking area, both the Middle Fork and West Fork trails are accessed west along a four-wheel drive road beneath the power lines. Just a few hundred yards in is the junction where Middle Fork Trail turns south. Cross the bridge, and the trail starts its ascent (a steep four-wheel drive road also leads to Middle Fork Lake) on the east side of the river. It's a fairly gradual, 1-mile climb through the spruce-fir vegetation to the junction with Lost Lake Trail #91, which leads 4 miles southeast to Lost Lake. Middle Fork Lake is 1 mile to the southwest.

Just beyond this junction Middle Fork Trail crosses a waterfall and climbs more steeply in a series of switchbacks to the lake, which sits below the 12,000 foot peaks to the southwest (Frazier Mountain is directly across the lake). Middle Fork Lake was also dammed to provide water for the Big Ditch, which is visible alongside the trail just before the waterfall.

LOST LAKE TRAIL #91:
4 miles   Moderate   Elevation: 9,600-11,500 feet

Accessed from Middle Fork Lake Trail, Lost Lake Trail climbs 4 miles to Lost Lake and East Fork River Trail. Take SH 150 south out of Red River 6 miles to the end of the pavement. Follow FR 58 west to the Middle Fork-West Fork parking area, and follow this access trail a few hundred yards further west to the junction of the Middle Fork Trail. Turn south across the river and follow Middle Fork Lake Trail for a 1-mile climb to the Lost Lake Trail junction.

Turn left (east) to follow Lost Lake Trail as it begins a series of long switchbacks up the side of the canyon above the river in a fairly gradual ascent, similar to both Middle Fork and East Fork Trails. Over your shoulder views of Bull-of-the-Woods ridge appear along the climb, and up ahead views of the high peaks surrounding Wheeler appear on the horizon.

The rest of the hike follows the edge of the ridge as you climb south toward the wilderness boundary, about 1.5 miles from Lost Lake. At the end of the switchbacks a clearing provides a view of the entire Red River Valley. This is indeed the high country, with dense, alpine vegetation covering the ground and 13,000-foot peaks rising ahead. The old Lost Lake Trail you passed on East Fork Trail intersects the trail less than 1 mile before the lake, and once past the dam site, Lost Lake sparkles in a basin ringed by

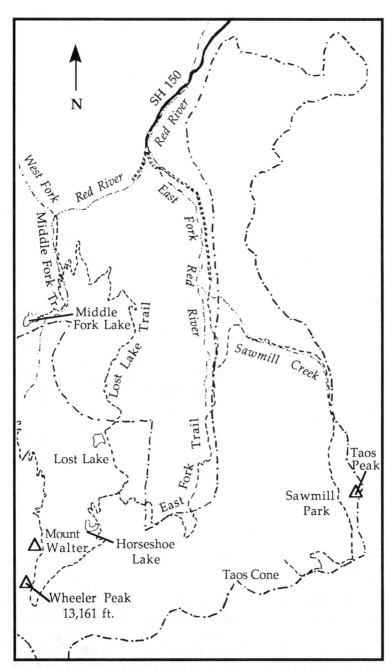

LOST LAKE TRAIL #91

Wheeler and its neighboring 13,000-foot peaks. East Fork Trail continues south from the lake to the junction with Horseshoe Lake or back down the East Fork of Red River to SH 150. Again, you should avoid camping in the lake basin to protect the fragile stream-side vegetation and avoid polluting the lake.

WEST FORK RIVER TRAIL #58:
3 miles   Moderate   Elevation: 9,500-10,800 feet

This trail is not in the wilderness, but is also accessed off SH 150 at the Middle Fork and Lost Lake Trails junction, providing a route to the Taos Ski Valley or Wheeler Peak. Follow SH 150 6 miles out of Red River to the end of the pavement, then west along the dirt road to the parking area for Middle Fork and West Fork Trails. A few hundred yards further along the four-wheel drive road is the turnoff to Middle Fork Lake and Lost Lake Trails. Cross under the gate and continue along the road to access West Fork Trail.

The road is a gradual ascent as it follows the powerline through this pocket of private land along the river. The road periodically leaves the powerline as it follows the West Fork through a meadow area, then past a boarded up cabin. At about .75 miles, the power line turns sharply west to ascend the ridge towards Bull-of-the-Woods, and the road winds around to the northwest (right). Raspberries grow all along the path and are usually ripe by late August. Views of the valley open up behind you.

The road steepens as it begins to narrow to a trail, and a broken sign at the foot of a post indicates that the trail bears left, towards the river, while the road circles around to the right. Follow the trail across the slope to the river crossing and continue up into the trees. A short distance uphill another signless post stands at what looks like a trail junction; bear right, up through the trees. There is considerable downfall here, and you have to look carefully to find the trail as it switchbacks up the hill.

After about .5 miles, the trail reaches the power easement (old poles are still standing) and heads south up the easement towards Bull-of-the-Woods. It's a short but steep climb to Bull-of-the-Woods Meadow, a large pasture full of yarrow and fringed gentians. The trail skirts the meadow to the west, past a horse corral, to a campsite near a small pond and the junction with the trails heading to Wheeler Peak, Gold Hill, and the Taos Ski Valley. Gold

Hill Trail #64 heads northwest 3 miles to Gold Hill and Goose Lake; Bull-of-the-Woods Trail heads 2 miles west down to the Taos Ski Valley; and Crest Ridge Trail #90 (Old Mike Peak Trail) heads south 5 miles to Wheeler Peak. Climb a little ways up Trail #90 for a view of both the Taos Ski Valley to the west and the Red River Valley to the east.

Thick spruce-fir forest above Red River

Taos Ski Valley Access

Access to the Wheeler Peak Wilderness from the west is via the Taos Ski Valley. This area is called Twining and is full of old mining routes and sites. Most people use Williams Lake Trail to climb the west side of Wheeler Peak, but you can also get to the peak via Bull-of-the-Woods Trail. To reach the ski basin travel north of Taos on SH 522 to SH 150. Turn east for 15 miles where the road dead ends at the Taos Ski Valley.

Mark and Jakob at Bull-of-the-Woods Pasture

BULL-OF-THE-WOODS TRAIL #58:
2 miles   Difficult   Elevation: 9,500-11,500 feet

Bull-of-the-Woods Trail begins at the northeast corner of the Taos Ski Valley where the road turns south to the private home area and Williams Lake Trail. Bull-of-the-Woods heads straight uphill to the east on the north side of East Fork Rio Hondo and the south side of the power line. Maintain an easterly course as the trail crosses several power line openings until you reach the last pole. Follow the arrow pointing left, up a short hill, where the trail turns northeast again as it follows the creek.

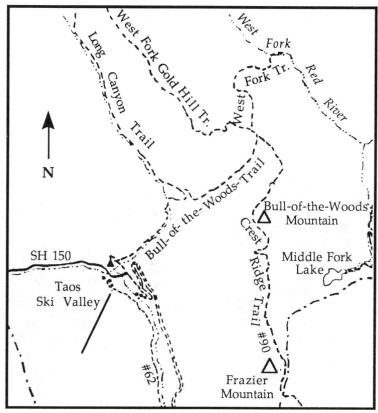

West Fork

Fork

West Fork Gold Hill Tr.

Long Canyon Trail

West Fork Tr.

Red River

N

Bull-of-the-Woods Trail

Bull-of-the-Woods Mountain

Crest Ridge Trail #90

SH 150

Middle Fork Lake

Taos Ski Valley

#62

Frazier Mountain

BULL-OF-THE-WOODS TRAIL #58

At about 1 mile the trail crosses a forest road; signs indicate the junction with Columbine-Twining National Recreation Trail to the northwest (left). Long Canyon Trail leads 4.5 miles to Gold Hill and 13 miles to Columbine Campground.

Bull-of-the-Woods continues to the northeast (right). Follow the arrow up through the trees to where the road turns north and climbs to another set of arrows on the trees: the arrow to the left points out a shortcut back to the ski valley; the arrow to the right points out the road switchback to the south. Follow the switchback south, and at the top of the hill you can see down over the valley to the Taos llano. The road then turns back northeast in a direct ascent to Bull-of-the-Woods Pasture, a large grassy area, at the top of the ridge. There is a good campsite near a small pond at the south end of the meadow. Gold Hill Trail #64 heads northwest 3 miles to Gold Hill and Goose Lake. West Fork River Trail, which leads 3 miles down to FR 58 on the Red River side of the wilderness, heads north across the meadow. Crest Ridge Trail #90 follows the road south along the ridge to Bull-of-the-Woods Mountain and on to Wheeler Peak, 6 miles. Climb Trail #90 a little ways to a view of both the Taos Ski Valley to the west and the Red River Valley to the east.

View east to the Red River Valley from Crest Ridge Trail

CREST RIDGE TRAIL #90: (Bull-of-the-Woods to Wheeler Peak)
6 miles   Difficult   Elevation: 10,000-13,161 ft.

This trail follows the crest ridgeline of the wilderness from Bull-of-the-Woods Pasture to Wheeler Peak. Because of its elevation and exposure, this hike should be attempted only in fair weather unless you come prepared for alpine conditions.

From Bull-of-the-Woods Pasture follow the old mining road southeast up to the top of the ridge where you can see north into the Red River Valley and south to the slopes of the Taos Ski Valley. Continue south along the road, bearing left where the road forks.

The road narrows to a trail, and at about 1.5 miles enters the wilderness along the west side of the ridge. Another .5 miles along the trail you cross Frazer Mountain at 12,163 feet. The trail drops down into a forested area in the La Cal Basin where you can find shelter to camp if you prefer to ascend Wheeler in the

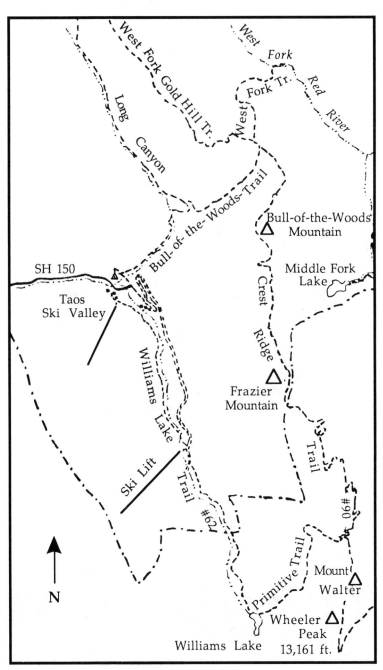

CREST RIDGE TRAIL #90

early part of the next day.

Mt. Walter, over 13,000 feet, is the next peak crossed, and less than half a mile later you reach the short trail to the right that climbs to the summit of Wheeler Peak at 13,161 feet. This highest New Mexico Mountain is named for Major George M. Wheeler who surveyed and collected geologic and biologic material on the mountain. Watch the weather closely while you're on the summit so you don't get caught in inclement weather.

WILLIAMS LAKE TRAIL #62:
4.5 miles   Difficult   Elevation: 9,400-11,000 feet

This is the route, via Williams Lake Trail, that most hikers take on their way to Wheeler Peak. Williams Lake sits in a glacial cirque 4.5 miles from the Taos Ski Valley.

The trail begins at the east end of the ski valley parking lot at the termination of SH 150. Turn south and follow a road through the condominium and cabin area. This road is accessible to cars during the summer, but must be skied during snow season. The third switchback leads north through private land to Bull-of-the-Woods Trail; stay on the main road until you see the sign stating that this is private land and unauthorized vehicles are not permitted beyond this point.

From here the road continues to climb for 1.5 miles to the midway restaurant and Kachina Chairlift. The high wilderness peaks loom ahead. At the restaurant, continue south along the Rio Hondo a short distance to where the road forks; bear southeast along the stream, as the road to the right turns and circles back to the chairlift. About .5 miles up, the road narrows to a trail, and a marker indicates that Williams Lake is 2 miles farther.

The trail leaves the stream and continues its southeast climb through the trees to a meadow. Behind you appear the high peaks of the Gold Hill area, and Kachina Peak is the mountain to the west. The trail passes through boulder fields and east-side talus slopes to the Wheeler Peak Wilderness boundary sign, about 1 mile from the restaurant. From here it's a steady climb through the trees to the saddle above Williams Lake. Camping is restricted around the lake to preserve the shoreline. From the lake it's 1.4 miles up a primitive trail to Wheeler Peak.

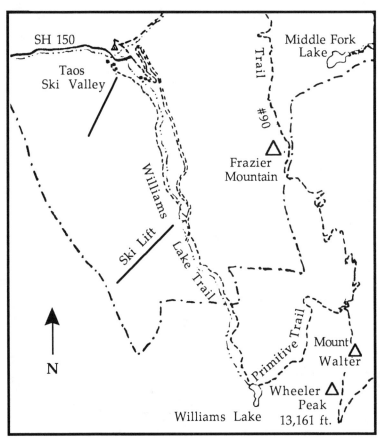

WILLIAMS LAKE TRAIL #62

Section III. Pecos Wilderness

The huge Pecos Wilderness, 233,667 acres, is probably the most popular of the northern New Mexico wilderness areas. People speak with awe of the Pecos—its size, its 12,000 foot peaks, its wild rivers and alpine lakes, its dense forests and abundant wildlife—but they have not treated the area with such respect. Consequently, the Forest Service has had to periodically monitor and restrict use of the wilderness. A permit system was established in 1973 to track numbers of visitors in areas of high use; while permits are no longer required, most of the lakes and some stream sections are closed to overnight use.

Perhaps the most remarkable aspect of the Pecos is the fact that there *is* a Pecos Wilderness at all, considering the depredation that occurred in these mountains during the 19th century's rush to conquer the West. Until the beginning of that century, the Indian and Hispanic people living in the mountains had used the forests for sustenance: gathering fuel wood, hunting the prolific populations of deer, elk, bear, and mountain lion, grazing their sheep. While some of the grazing and timbering practices employed by the local villagers caused erosion and pollution problems, most of this was on a relatively small scale. Then came the Anglos, and their mining, timbering, trapping, hunting, and grazing activities took a devastating toll on the Pecos' natural resources between the years of 1820 and 1920. Beavers were eliminated from a mountain stream in a matter of days; mining tents sprang up like dandelions after the first tale of gold nuggets; native grasses and wildflowers were devoured or trampled by hundreds of head of sheep and cattle; tens of thousands of high country acres were stripped of trees to supply the Santa Barbara Tie and Pole Company.

Fortunately, the 20th century produced people who looked at the mountains of the Pecos and saw not dollar signs on trees and cows, but the beauty and ecological importance of diverse forests, wildlife, free-flowing streams, and healthy mountain meadows. Some of these people sparked the creation of the Forest Reserves, which in turn became the National Forest of the Department of Agriculture. While everyone agreed that the rapaciousness of the private sector had to be restrained in these national forests, there was some disagreement as to whether these forests should resemble national parks, dedicated to the preservation of natural beauty and wildlife, or should be "working" forests managed for long-term production of timber and other resources. Under the guidance of Gifford Pinchot, appointed by Teddy Roosevelt, the latter philosophy held sway, and the groundwork for today's "multiple use" management was laid down.

While the Pecos lands have experienced a fantastic recovery from the rape of the 19th century, periodic Forest Service management decisions still bring back those insidious memories of falling trees, washed away slopes, and silt-filled creeks. Citizens are protective of their Pecos and let the Forest Service know when those memories are awakened by the prospect of a road from Terrero across the Pecos high country east to Las Vegas (proposed in the 1970's) or the Elk Mountain timber sale currently under appeal (1991). The Pecos has meant and means many things to many people. But once you put on your pack and leave the Santa Fe Ski Basin for the aspen groves and tumbling waters of the Rio Nambe, or climb from Iron Gate Campground to the lush meadow of Hamilton Mesa, the Pecos means wilderness to you. And what awaits you at Truchas Peak or Pecos Falls will tell you that in wildness is truly the preservation of the world, as Thoreau said.

Access to the Pecos Wilderness is via the towns of Las Vegas and Mora from the east, the village of Pecos on the south, the Santa Fe Ski Basin on the southwest, and north from Española to Peñasco.

Santa Fe Ski Basin Access

This central area of the Pecos sees the most use, both summer and winter, because of its accessibility from Santa Fe. Winsor Trail begins right at the end of Hyde Park Road (SH 475) at the Santa Fe Ski Basin and is heavily traveled to Santa Fe Baldy and the western lakes, Katherine and Spirit. But the scenery and terrain are gorgeous, and you can quickly get away from these more heavily traveled areas into the high country around Horsethief Meadow and Pecos Baldy. Hyde Park Road leads north from Santa Fe 15 miles to the ski basin.

WINSOR TRAIL #254 (Santa Fe Ski Basin to Spirit Lake):
7 miles   Moderate   Elevation: 10,400-10,800 feet

While Winsor Trail actually originates on the highway near Bishop's Lodge, most hikers pick it up where it reaches the ski basin and enters the wilderness 1 mile up the ridge. A main artery of the Pecos, the trail goes all the way to Cowles and accesses many of the other trails on both the Santa Fe and Pecos sides of the wilderness. Park in the ski basin lower parking lot, and pick up the trail beginning on the north side across the Little Tesuque Creek.

The first .5 miles to the wilderness boundary is a tough climb with a 40-pound pack, but once achieved, the rest of the trail is quite a bit easier. The lower switchbacks are short and steep as the trail climbs along the power line meadow. Several longer east-west climbs bring you to the top of the ridge at the boundary. From there the trail quickly drops onto the north side of the ridge to the valley behind the ski basin. Long views extend north and west to the Jemez and Sangres at periodic breaks in the thick conifer forest. The junction with Trail #403, which leads 1.75 miles to Rio Nambe Trail, is .5 miles from the wilderness boundary.

Winsor Trail turns south through an aspen grove to the north side of the ski basin below Lake and Penitente Peaks. Here the Nambe Lake Trail climbs southeast to the lake. Cross the creek, and more aspen groves line the path as Winsor Trail travels east toward Santa Fe Baldy, looming ahead. You'll pass the La Vega shortcut, which also leads to Rio Nambe Trail. Winsor continues

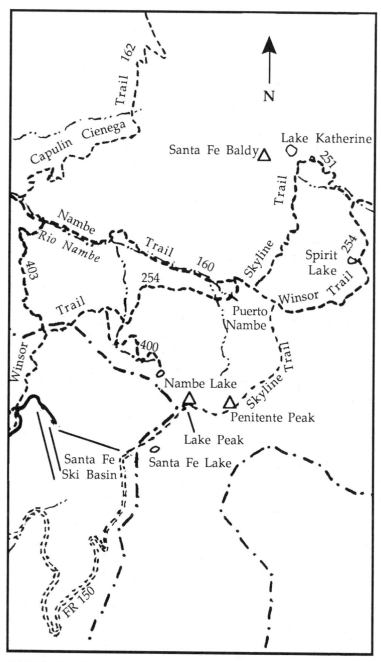

WINSOR TRAIL #254 (Santa Fe Ski Basin to Spirit
Lake)

on to a small meadow on the side of the ridge directly below Baldy, where the trail turns south again back into the trees and climbs to several streams of the Rio Nambe. Cross the streams and follow the switchbacks northeast across the open slopes to the top of the ridge. Here the trail turns southeast and climbs along the top of the ridge to Puerto Nambe in the meadow below Santa Fe Baldy.

The trail divides here: Winsor continues 2 miles to Spirit Lake, while Sky Line Trail #251 leads 3 miles north to Lake Katherine. This is the crossroads of the Pecos—follow Winsor Trail as it leads to Spirit Lake. Turn east (right) along level terrain through Puerto Nambe meadow. It's only about .5 miles to the continuation of Skyline Trail (#251) south (right) to Lake and Penitente Peaks. Winsor Trail continues northeast down into a canyon on the Cowles side of the Pecos—through the trees you can see over the Pecos River to Hamilton Mesa and Mora Flats. The trail stays in spruce-fir vegetation along an easy downhill route, 1.5 miles to the Spirit Lake Basin. The smallest of the Pecos Lakes, Spirit is fed by underground springs and is quite shallow, but full of jumping brookies. We've seen 40 fish pulled out in a matter of hours, but mercifully thrown back, in keeping with the Native American sacredness of this body of water, where the "spirits" of the most powerful Indian medicine men reside. Camping is prohibited within the lake basin, as with all the Pecos lakes.

Winsor Trail continues north, downhill another .25 miles to Winsor Creek, beyond which lies the junction with Skyline Trail #251. This trail leads 2 miles west (left), uphill to Lake Katherine and 2 miles east (right) to Stewart Lake.

SKYLINE TRAIL #251, #254 (Aspen Basin to Puerto Nambe):
4 miles   Difficult   Elevation: 10,400-12,404 feet (at Lake Peak)

Skyline Trail is the longest trail in the Pecos if you were to follow it in its entirety from Tesuque Peak to the Las Vegas side of the wilderness. This description follows the trail from its west side trailhead at Tesuque Peak to Puerto Nambe. To reach the trailhead you can either hike FR 150 from Aspen Vista Campground (6 miles) or climb up the ski basin slopes to the top of the ski runs at Tesuque Peak. The easiest way up is to follow the ski basin service road that starts on the east side of the ski area and climbs to the midway restaurant, then continues to the top of the

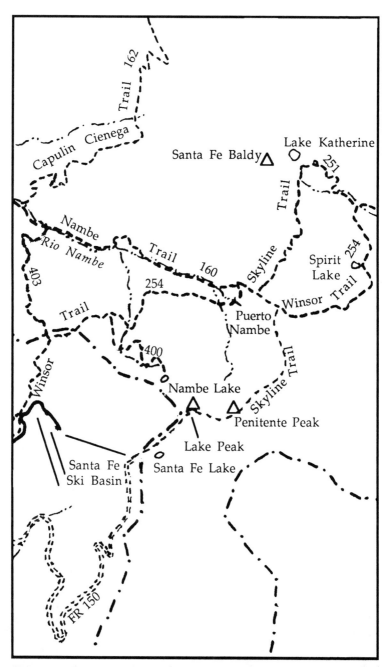

SKYLINE TRAIL #251 (Aspen Basin to Puerto Nambe)

middle chairlift. Here it turns north and along increasingly steep terrain climbs to the radio towers at the top of Tesuque Peak. Just before you reach the towers, the service road meets FR 150 in its ascent from Aspen Vista Campground. Turn left, follow the forest road almost to the towers, and Trail #251 begins to the north (left) where a ski trail descends the mountain. This climb to the towers is approximately 2 miles.

Follow the trail north, into the wilderness, and it's a short hike through the trees to the open slopes of Lake Peak. The trail disappears in the fragile alpine terrain, but continue straight up the peak to a truly spectacular 360 degree view: to the north loom the Truchas Peaks; to the west, Santa Fe Baldy rises above Puerto Nambe: to the south, the Jemez and Sandia Mountains define the horizon; and to the east, the huge Pecos River drainage circles the wilderness.

Trail #251 follows a precipitous route along the top of the ridge extending from Lake Peak to Penitente Peak, full of precarious climbs along narrow rock ledges. To the northwest you can see down into the Nambe Lake basin (accessed off Winsor Trail) and southeast into the Santa Fe Lake basin. Lake Peak is one of the sacred peaks that demarcate the boundaries of the homeland of the Pueblo Indians, and Nambe Lake was once the site of tribal fertility rituals. The trail continues northeast along the ridge to Penitente Peak, and descends to a saddle between the two peaks, where you can then climb Penitente Peak or circle the peak to the south. Once beyond the peak you'll enter the trees again and make several switchbacks down the ridge (at the end of the last switchback you can look back up at the peaks you just crossed) to the last leg of the trail heading north to the junction with Winsor Trail. At the junction turn left, and Puerto Nambe lies about .5 miles to the west. To the right, Winsor Trail #254 leads to Spirit Lake. To make a loop hike, follow Winsor Trail from Puerto Nambe back to the ski basin.

The first time I ever did this hike we did everything wrong. First, we went in August, when it was inevitable that a lightning storm would arise in the afternoon to prevent us from crossing the open ridge between the two peaks. Second, we did the hike backwards, hiking up Winsor Trail from the ski basin to Puerto Nambe, then up to Penitente Peak. If we'd climbed the ski basin first and crossed the peaks in the morning we would have made it. The hike was aborted (one of us forgot our rain poncho as well!) and a lesson learned, so be sure to pick the right season and the right route if you want to make a loop hike.

SKYLINE TRAIL #251 (Puerto Nambe to Lake Katherine):
3 miles   Moderate   Elevation: 11,000-12,000 feet

At the Puerto Nambe crossroads, Winsor Trail #254 continues northeast to Spirit Lake, while Trail #251 heads north to one of the highest and most popular destinations in the Pecos—Lake Katherine. At an almost 12,000-foot elevation, this largest of the Pecos lakes sees 50 people on a weekend, both backpackers and day hikers willing to make the long trek in from either Cowles or the Santa Fe Ski Basin.

At Puerto Nambe, follow Trail #251 north as it begins the climb toward the saddle below Santa Fe Baldy. Long switchbacks take you through the lower meadow area and up onto the ridge where sweeping views of the Jemez Mountains can be seen to the west. At the saddle, with Santa Fe Baldy right there in front of you, the trail immediately drops over onto the Cowles side of the wilderness, where suddenly you have sweeping views east to the Pecos River Valley. A series of short switchbacks across treeless terrain takes you down to the head of the canyon you'll traverse northwest to the lake. Lush vegetation intermingled with boulders and scree slopes make this a beautiful hike. The trail leads about .75 miles to the lake basin, where you climb across a boulder field bordering the south side of the lake to pick up the continuation of Trail #251. The lake itself, the largest of the Pecos lakes, sits just below Baldy, surrounded by boulder fields and fragile vegetation on the steep slopes of the lake basin. Trail #251 continues 2 miles to the junction with Trail #254 to Spirit Lake (.5 miles) while #251 continues on to Stewart Lake (2 miles).

SKYLINE TRAIL #251 (Spirit Lake To Lake Katherine):
3 miles   Difficult   Elevation: 10,800-12,000 feet

Trail #254 leads north from Spirit Lake to the junction with Skyline Trail #251, which goes to Lake Katherine to the west and Stewart Lake to the northeast. The trail from Spirit is mostly downhill, about .25 miles, to the headwaters of Winsor Creek. Cross the stream and the junction to Lake Katherine is just a short distance from the stream. Turn west and prepare for a long,

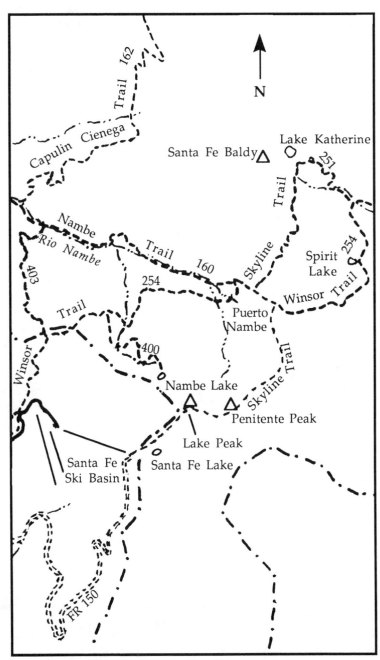

SKYLINE TRAIL #251 (Spirit Lake to Lake
Katherine; Puerto Nambe to Lake Katherine)

steady, uphill climb. Although the climb is fairly arduous, the trail periodically levels out, so you can catch your breath. Through the trees to the north you can discern the Santa Barbara Divide and the Truchas Peaks. A series of switchbacks takes you to a long, steady ascent along the north side of a canyon, which levels out at a stream next to the last campsite outside of the lake basin. The boulder fields surrounding the lake become visible, and sebadillosos and cow parsnip proliferate. A small pond lies below the lake where the trail climbs across a scree slope, then reaches the lake in its spectacular basin setting below Santa Fe Baldy. Camping is prohibited in this high alpine, fragile setting, but many hikers make Lake Katherine their destination from either Cowles or the Santa Fe Ski Basin. Trail #251 continues on to Puerto Nambe, about 3 miles up across the saddle below Santa Fe Baldy.

Pecos Access

Many Pecos Wilderness Trails are accessed from the little town of Cowles, which lies on SH 63 about 20 miles north of Pecos. FR 223, about 1 mile south of Cowles, leads 4 miles to Iron Gate Campground, which accesses the eastern side of the Pecos from the Hamilton Mesa and Mora Flats area to the Eastern Divide. Jack's Creek Campground, at the termination of SH 63, provides wilderness parking and access to the central Pecos Baldy area. The easternmost trailhead of Winsor Trail begins in Winsor Campground, 1 mile west of Cowles, and leads to the Stewart Lake area. Panchuela Campground, 2 miles from Cowles, accesses the Cave Creek area and connects to many central wilderness trails.

HAMILTON MESA TRAIL #249, #260 (Iron Gate Campground to Beatty's Flats):
5.5 miles   Moderate   Elevation: 9,350-9,400 feet

This hike, northeast out of Iron Gate Campground, is a wonderful introduction to hiking in the Pecos: moderate terrain for the neophyte backpacker, breathtaking views of the high Pecos peaks, plenty of water, and a diverse landscape of meadow and mixed conifer forest. Follow SH 63 north out of Pecos to the Iron Gate Campground access road, about 1 mile before Cowles. This road leads 4 miles east to the campground.

Hamilton Mesa Trail enters the Pecos Wilderness at the north end of the campground and climbs gently east about .5 miles along the ridge above the Mora River, affording views east, to the junction with Mora Flats Trail #250. Hamilton Mesa Trail veers off to the north, climbing a ridge up to the mesa. Hamilton Mesa is one of the most beautiful in the Pecos. Groves of aspen trees dot the landscape, and wildflowers bloom in abundance—wild iris, spiderwort, cinquefoil. The trail heads north across the mesa, and to the west loom the Pecos peaks from Penitente to the Truchas Peaks.

After several miles along the mesa you reach the junction with Beatty's Trail #260 (Hamilton Mesa Trail continues on to Pecos Falls), which turns west into the mixed conifer forest. The trail is mostly downhill as it descends to the Pecos River. At about 1 mile is the junction with Trail #270 which turns north and eventually circles back around to Hamilton Mesa. Beatty's Trail continues

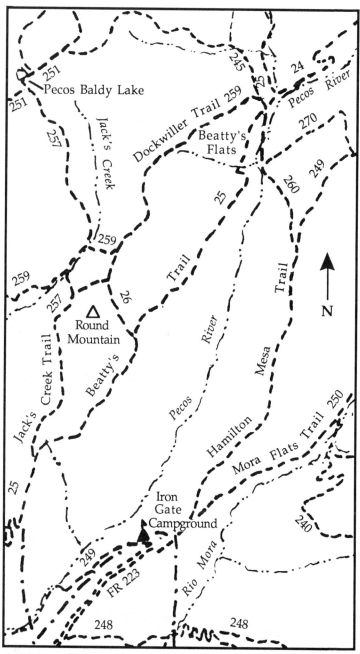

HAMILTON MESA TRAIL #249, #260 (Iron Gate Campground to Beatty's Flats)

another .5 miles north to the river. A foot bridge leads across the fast flowing Pecos to the Flats area, where signs tell you that camping is prohibited from this bridge north along the river to the next bridge. The meadow area above the river is named for George Beatty, an infamous gold miner whose original cabin once sat in these meadows on the north side of the fence (the existing cabins which sit on the ridge directly west are Forest Service and Game and Fish administrative sites).

From Beatty's Flats several trails lead to Jack's Creek Campground (Beatty's Trail #25, 7 miles southwest); to the Santa Barbara Divide (Pecos Trail #24, 5 miles north); and to Pecos Baldy Lake (Sebadillosos Trail #245, 2.5 miles west).

SEBADILLOSOS TRAIL #245, #257 (Beatty's Flats To Pecos Baldy Lake):
2.5 miles   Difficult   Elevation: 9,400-11,600 feet

Named in Spanish for the ubiquitous skunk cabbage that grows along the trail, Sebadillosos Trail is the most direct, but steepest route to the Trailrider Wall-Pecos Baldy Lake area. At Beatty's Flats cross the Pecos River to the west side, and a little ways up the ridge is a sign that indicates Trail #245 to Pecos Baldy Lake. Here, also, Beatty's Trail #25 heads south to Jack's Creek Campground, and Pecos Falls Trail #24 leads north to the Santa Barbara Divide.

Follow the Trail #245 northwest up the ridge above the Forest Service administrative cabin site to the camping closure sign, where Trail #259 splits off south to Jack's Creek Campground. Stay to the right on Sebadillosos Trail, which climbs uphill through forested terrain and fields of skunk cabbage until the descent to the Sebadillosos River, a beautiful creek crossed by stepping stones and a fallen log. On the other side of the river, the trail ascends through mixed conifer and across small springs that make portions of the trail wet and muddy (especially if you're behind a pack train).

After about .5 miles, the trail emerges into the meadows below the snowcapped ridge that indicates the final ascent to the Pecos Baldy area. The trail climbs steeply along the headwaters of the Sebadillosos River to the saddle between this canyon and the Rito Azul drainage. A sign indicates that Sebadillosos Trail ends here, at the junction with Jack's Creek Trail #257, which heads north

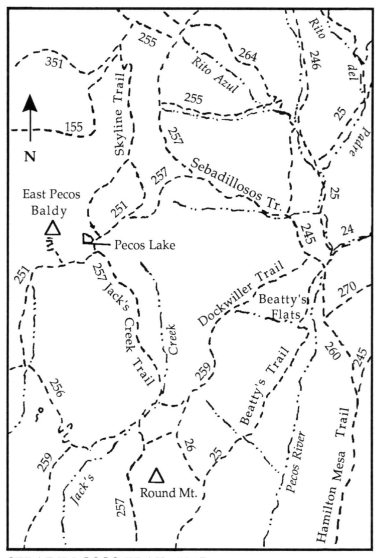

SEBADILLOSOS TRAIL #245

(right) to Trailrider's Wall and the Santa Barbara Divide. Continue on Trail #257, left, towards Pecos Baldy Lake, and suddenly, a little further past the sign, is your first view of the Divide in all its high country glory. You feel like you are close to the top of the world. Behind you, Hamilton Mesa and the Pecos River Valley show where you've been.

The trail starts a traverse of the ridge, east to west. If it's early summer and the ridge is still snowcapped, you may have to scramble along the old trail below the newer trail that angles over the ridge to the plateau below Trailrider's Wall and follow a more horizontal route to avoid the snowfields. Be careful, as the ridge is precipitous, and a pack upsets your balance. Once over the ridge, circle back to the north to pick up the trail on top. Here in front of you will loom East Pecos Baldy with Trailrider's Wall stretching north. Now you *are* on top of the world.

Trail #257 merges with Skyline Trail #251, which heads north along Trailrider's Wall and south to Pecos Baldy Lake. It's .25 miles down the ridge south to Pecos Baldy Lake, which sits in a basin below East Pecos Baldy. Trail #251 continues southwest past East Pecos Baldy and Pecos Baldy 5 miles to Horsethief Meadow. Trail #257 continues pretty much due south to Jack's Creek Campground, 7.5. miles. Watch out for the Rocky Mountain bighorn sheep on the plateau and at the lake. This is their turf, and they assume any food in packs or tents is part of the territory. Quite tame, they will approach you looking for handouts (or lick you for salt). They seem to be in good shape, healthy and fit, and it's a pleasure to share a few hours with them.

View to Hamilton Mesa from Sebadillosos Trail

Pecos Falls

PECOS FALLS TRAIL #24 (Beatty's Flats to Pecos Falls):
4 miles Moderate Elevation: 9,400-10,400 feet

A moderate climb from Beatty's Flats to Pecos Falls, Trail #24 stays high on the aspen-covered ridge above the Pecos River. At Beatty's, cross over the bridge to the west side of the river and follow Trail #24 as it climbs a few hundred feet to the junction with Beatty's Trail #25, which leads south to Jack's Creek Campground and Sebadillosos Trail #245, which heads northwest to Trailrider's Wall and Pecos Baldy Lake. Continue north on Trail #24 above the river to a sign which reads: Pecos Falls 4, to the north; Pecos Baldy Lake 4, to the west; Iron Gate CG and Jack's Creek CG, to the south; and Truchas Lakes, to the northwest. This last arrow indicates the way to Beatty's Trail #25 heading north up the Rito del Padre to the Santa Barbara Divide. Stay on Trail #24 and continue north across the Rito del Padre and through the fence (please close the gate after you to keep the cows out of the Flats area). On this north side of the fence on the hillside above the river is the site of the original Beatty's Cabin.

Here the trail leaves the river (spur trails lead down to a large campsite on the riverbank) and switchbacks up the ridge west of the river. After the trail levels out near the top of the ridge, the climb becomes more gradual and meanders through beautiful aspen groves and mixed conifer forest. The trail stays on the east side of the ridge, and as it nears the junction with Jarosa Creek, it can become quite wet during spring and early summer—you might see the anemone windflower growing here.

Just before Jarosa Creek, Pecos Falls Trail #24 meets GasconTrail #239, and the trails merge (a spur trail leading down toward the Pecos River turns east before this junction and may cause some confusion). Follow the trail across Jarosa Creek as it descends to the Pecos River. Trail #24 then turns north (left) and continues to the Santa Barbara Divide; Trail #239 angles down the ridge to the river. You'll have to wade across the river to the grassy area below Trail #239 where Hamilton Mesa Trail #249 emerges from the south. Trail #239 continues 6.5 miles east to Gascon Point. Pecos Falls tumbles down the river rocks below the meadow (camping is prohibited here) into a series of pools, but the swiftness of the water—and the cold temperature—prevents leisurely bathing. It's a beautiful sight to behold, however.

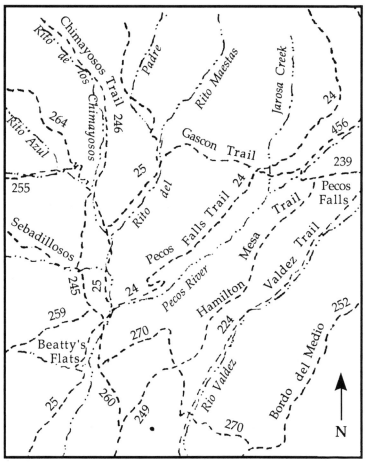

PECOS FALLS TRAIL #24 (Beatty's Flats to Pecos Falls)

HAMILTON MESA TRAIL #249 (Iron Gate Campground to Pecos Falls):
8 miles   Easy   Elevation: 9,350-10,400 feet

While you will probably see some day hikers on this trail hurrying along to the falls, take 2 or 3 days to enjoy the beauty of Hamilton Mesa and the falls. There are campsites along the mesa near seep springs and plenty of water once you reach the falls at the Pecos River.

The Truchas Peaks from Hamilton Mesa Trail

Take SH 63 out of the village of Pecos towards Cowles; turn off at FR 223 to Iron Gate Campground (4 miles). Hamilton Mesa Trail begins at the north end of the campground and climbs gently for about .5 miles above the Rio Mora canyon to the junction with Trail #250, which leads right (east) to Mora Flats. Stay on Trail #249 to the left, and its about a 1-mile climb up to Hamilton Mesa.

Once on the mesa the trail levels out as you hike through alpine meadows interspersed with stands of mixed conifer. In the spring, wild iris and golden pea bloom in profusion, along with spiderwort, cinquefoil and bluebells. Views extend from the peaks near Santa Fe to the Truchas Peaks and Chimayosos Peak near the Santa Barbara Divide.

At about 3 miles you reach the junction with Trail #260 to Beatty's Flats, heading left (west) 2.5 miles. Continue north on Trail #249, past a seep spring, through more spectacular mountain meadows. A spur trail out to the top of the mesa turns sharply right, while the main trail continues north. At about 4 miles you pass Trail #270, which also leads left (west) to Beatty's, and just a little further up the trail, it heads right (east) to the Rio Valdez, about .5 miles away. Stay on Trail #249 as it heads out of the trees, and a beautiful campsite is available just up the hill from the trail

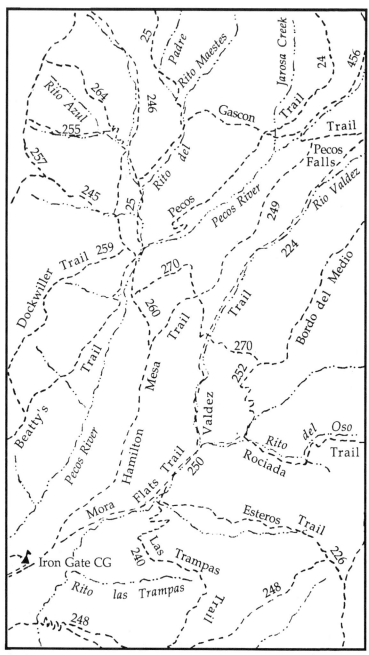

HAMILTON MESA TRAIL #249 (Iron Gate Campground to Pecos Falls)

(a seep spring on Trail #270 provides water).

Hamilton Mesa Trail continues across the meadow and enters a stand of conifer, where the trail climbs a little as it emerges again into a meadow where you can see down to the Rio Valdez. The trail then reenters the forest, staying in the trees the last 2 miles to the falls. The terrain is mostly level, although a short section loses elevation, before the last level .5 miles to the falls.

The trail enters a lovely meadow just above Pecos Falls where Gascon Trail #239 continues east to the Rio Valdez and west across the Pecos River to Pecos Trail #24 leading north to the Santa Barbara Divide and south to Beatty's. Camping is prohibited in the fragile meadow, so plan your trip with time to continue on Trail #239 or back down #249 to a campsite. The falls tumbles down the rocks below the river crossing where spur trails lead down to the pool below.

MORA FLATS TRAIL #250 (Iron Gate Campground to Mora Flats)
3 miles   Moderate   Elevation: 9,350-9,400 feet

This is another easy hike out of Iron Gate Campground to lovely campsites along the Rio Mora. This trail also provides access to the more lightly used east side of the Pecos. Take SH 63 north out of the village of Pecos past Terrero to the turnoff to Iron Gate Campground, FR 223. This rough dirt road leads 4 miles to the campground.

To reach the Mora Flats Trail, take Hamilton Mesa Trail #249 at the north end of the campground and follow it for an easy .5 miles to where the trails intersect. Trail #249 heads north across Hamilton Mesa to Pecos Falls, while Trail #250 continues east above the Rio Mora. The trail gradually descends to the river through ponderosa pine and stands of aspen; golden pea, wild rose, cinquefoil, and penstemon color the way. Periodically you can catch glimpses of the river below.

You pass through a fence and begin to see the area called the Flats below—long, narrow meadows alongside the river. A sign asks you to stay on the newer trail down to the flats, which stays up on the hillside for another .5 miles before a long switchback takes you down to the river. There are obvious campsites alongside the river, where the blue and white columbine, state flower of Colorado, grows along the banks. Remember to reuse a fire ring if

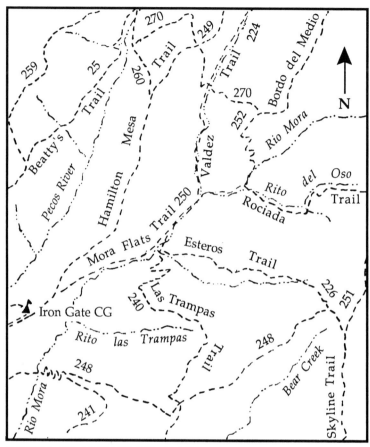

MORA FLATS TRAIL # 250

it's been left rather than disturb a new site, and try not to destroy the fragile streamside vegetation.

At the sign that indicates the continuation of Trail #250 a spur trail heads east through the clearing and across the Rio Mora. This is Esteros Trail #226, which leads 5 miles to Spring Mountain and also accesses Las Trampas Trail #240. Mora Flats Trail continues east to the north end of the flats where Valdez Trail #224 turns north along the Rio Valdez. Trail #250 crosses the Rio Mora and continues east to the Eastern Divide.

VALDEZ TRAIL #224 (Mora Flats to Gascon Trail):
9 miles   Moderate   Elevation: 9,300-11,800 feet

This trail provides a wet but less traveled route from Mora Flats to the Santa Barbara Divide, deep in the canyon of the Rio Valdez. Because of its length, the ascent is only moderately steep, and water and campsites are available the entire route.

To find the trail, take Mora Flats Trail #250 east from Iron Gate Campground (via Trail #249, as described in the previous section). At the north end of the flats the Rio Valdez and Rio Mora merge, and Valdez Trail turns along the west side of the Rio Valdez, while Trail #250 crosses over and continues along the Rio Mora. The meadow soon narrows, and the first of many river crossings is encountered. We had quite an adventure on this trail in early summer during high run-off and found ourselves walking across fallen log bridges over raging torrents of water and fording rapids hanging on to staffs and tree branches for dear life. So wait until after the snow melt, in mid-to-late June, before hiking this trail.

The first several miles to the junction with Trail #270 is through a narrow, forested canyon with four river crossings. You'll have to wade across if you have a fear of balancing on logs, although you can avoid the third crossing by staying on the west

The raging Rio Valdez

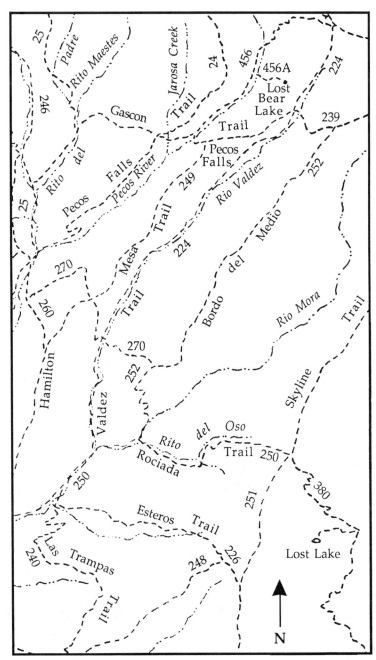

VALDEZ TRAIL #224 (Mora Flats to Gascon Trail)

side of the river and bushwacking your way to the next crossing, not far away. A sign at the trail junction points left to Beatty's, Trail #270, and straight ahead to Skyline Trail #251. Trail #270 climbs steeply up the side of the canyon for about .5 miles to the top of Hamilton Mesa where it meets Hamilton Mesa Trail #249 just above the seep spring in a grove of trees. Valdez Trail #224 continues north past the barely discernible continuation of Trail #270 east to Bordo del Medio (the ridge between the Valdez and the Rio Mora). After two more river crossings the trail stays on the west bank of the Rio Valdez through meadows full of good campsites. You can see a section of Hamilton Mesa Trail on the ridge above you before the trail starts to climb through the trees high above the Rio Valdez. This 2 miles of the trail is steeper, through mixed conifer forest, until the trail descends again to the river in a large marshy area full of gentians and marsh marigold. The trail once again climbs up above the river and continues north to the junction with Gascon Trail #239. Here the trails merge for a short distance to the west until Trail #224 continues north toward Santa Barbara Divide. Trail #239 continues west to Pecos Falls or east to Gascon Point out of Las Vegas.

TRAIL #270 (Rio Valdez to Beatty's Flats):
3 miles   Difficult   Elevation: 9,600-10,000 feet

Trail #270 provides a more lightly used route on the east side of the Pecos from the Rio Valdez, across Hamilton Mesa, and down to Beatty's Flats. Sections of the trail are quite steep and wet, making travel difficult.

The #270 trail junction is found about 2 miles up Valdez Trail from Mora Flats. A sign there points to Beatty's to the northwest and Skyline Trail along the continuation of Valdez Trail. Follow the arrow to Beatty's along Trail #270 as it begins a steep climb up the drainage above the Valdez through meadows and aspen groves. Flowing springs make this section of trail quite wet as it ascends Hamilton Mesa. At about .5 miles the trail turns more directly west, emerging at a seep spring just below Hamilton Mesa Trail #249. The trail continues a few hundred yards to the junction with Trail #249 in a stand of fir trees. Hamilton Mesa Trail continues north to Pecos Falls and south to Iron Gate Campground. To find the next section of Trail #270, turn south on Hamilton Mesa Trail and follow it just a few hundred yards to an

80

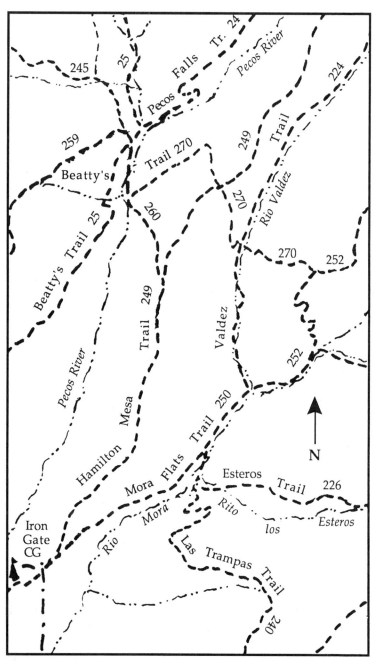

TRAIL #270

arrow-shaped sign in a fir tree indicating Beatty's Flats to the northwest.

This is the continuation of Trail #270, a 2-mile descent to Trail #260 near Beatty's Flats. The trail leads through mixed conifer forest interspersed with meadows while descending steeply. Also a wet route, you'll find the lovely magenta shooting star, blue-eyed grass, and the ubiquitous *sebadillosos*. As you near the junction with Trail #260, a portion of Trailrider's Wall comes into view. Trail #270 terminates at the junction with Trail #260, which leads north (right) .5 miles to Beatty's Flats and south (left) uphill to Hamilton Mesa Trail.

ROCIADA TRAIL #250 (Mora Flats to Eastern Divide):
5 miles   Difficult   Elevation: 9,400-11,300 feet

Rociada Trail leads from Mora Flats to the eastern side of the Pecos, also accessible from the town of Rociada outside of Las Vegas. Less traveled by people, and more traveled by ranchers bringing their cattle to graze in the central grasslands, this part of the Pecos offers lots of water, grassy hillsides, and views up and down the Eastern Divide.

To access Rociada Trail from Iron Gate Campground, take Hamilton Mesa Trail #249 east out of the campground to the junction with Trail #250 to Mora Flats (described in the MORA FLATS section). At the northeast end of the Flats, Valdez Trail #224 turns north to follow the Rio Valdez. This looks like the main trail, so be careful to turn east and continue along a smaller trail which leads back to the shore of the Rio Mora, which you must cross to continue on Trail #250. Another crossing brings you back to the north side of the river before the junction with Bordo del Medio Trail #252. This trail heads north across the ridge that separates the Rio Valdez and Rio Mora Valleys. Trail #250 immediately crosses the Mora again to follow a tributary, the Rito del Oso, as it continues east. The Rito del Oso was named for the trail bear camp set up by naturalist L.L. Dyche back in the late 1800's to trace the whereabouts of the grizzly bear, who once frequented the Pecos.

Rociada Trail begins a steep climb along rocky terrain out of the river canyon, crossing the south fork of the river before turning north to follow the north fork up to the Eastern Divide. The trail emerges into a large grassy area created by an old burn, where views extend to Hermit Peak to the east, and back over

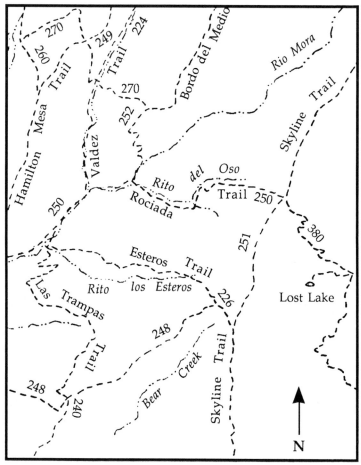

ROCIADA TRAIL #250 (Mora Flats to Skyline Trail)

your shoulder from Santa Fe Baldy to the Santa Barbara Divide. One-half mile further on, Rociada Trail meets Skyline Trail #251, which leads 7 miles north to Cebolla Peak and south along the divide to Spring Mountain and Elk Mountain. Rociada Trail continues east down the east side of the divide to Maestas Creek, and FR 276 out of Rociada.

SKYLINE TRAIL #251 (Rociada Trail to Cebolla Peak):
6 miles   Moderate   Elevation: 11,300-11,800 feet

This section of Skyline Trail is another trail that can be accessed from Iron Gate Campground or the village of Gascon out of Las Vegas. It follows the Eastern Divide from the junction of Rociada Trail #250 to Cebolla (onion) Mountain at the Gascon Trail junction.

To access the trail from Iron Gate Campground, take Hamilton Mesa Trail #249 east out of the campground to Mora Flats Trail #250. Follow this trail east along the Rio Mora to the Rito del Oso where it becomes Rociada Trail (as described in the previous section).

At the junction of Trail #250 and Trail #251 follow Skyline Trail north as it follows the divide through heavily forested areas as well as open meadows and boulder fields. Views extend in all directions from Hermit Peak to the south to the Santa Barbara Divide to the north. This part of Skyline Trail is a relatively easy walk through less traveled Pecos country.

The trail circles the west side of the wide, onion-shaped Cebolla Peak, the highest point on the Eastern Divide (11,879 feet), and intersects Gascon Trail just north of the peak. Gascon Trail #239 leads 4 miles west to Pecos Falls and 6 miles east across the divide to the town of Gascon.

JACK'S CREEK TRAIL #257, #25 (Jack's Creek Campground to Pecos Baldy Lake):
7.5 miles   Moderate   Elevation: 9,000-11,400 feet

This is one of the main arteries into the Pecos Wilderness and consequently sees a lot of use by both hikers and pack animals. It is the most direst route to the Pecos Baldy area and travels through some of the most beautiful Pecos country near Round Mountain.

Trail #257 is accessed off Beatty's Trail #25 which begins at the wilderness parking lot of Jack's Creek Campground, the termination of NM 63. Trail #25 heads north up the canyon via a series of steep switchbacks along a wide, well worn path. As the trail levels out after several miles, abundant wildflowers line the path: geranium, Jakob's ladder, golden pea, strawberries, thimbleberry.

As the trail begins to climb the vast meadows of Round Moun-

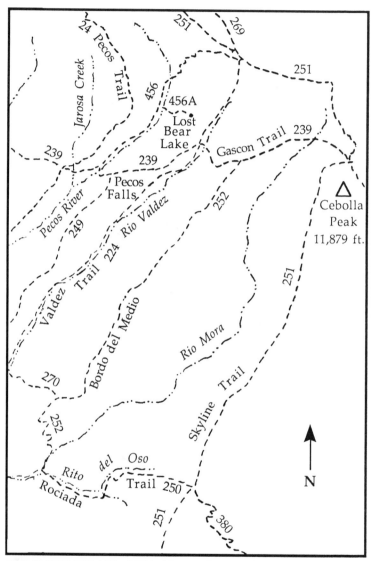

SKYLINE TRAIL #251 (Rociada Trail to Cebolla Peak)

tain it junctions with Jack's Creek Trail #257, the route to Pecos Baldy Lake. Beatty's Trail #25 continues to Beatty's Flats. Follow Trail #257 to the left, towards Round Mountain. Once into the mountain's meadows, the views of the Pecos peaks open up to the west, from Penitente and Lake Peaks to Pecos Baldy. The combination of the open meadow, dotted with aspen groves, and the distant high peaks is indicative of the diversity of terrain in the Pecos and one of the reasons it is so popular.

It's a slow, steady climb through the meadows of Round Mountain to the Jack's Creek crossing, where Dockwiller Trail #259 heads west to Panchuela Campground. Continue north across the river through this popular camping area. The junction with Trail #259 heading east to Beatty's Flats is just a little further up the river. It's only 1 more mile along a gentle ascent through the trees to Pecos Baldy Lake, a welcome respite below the towering East Pecos Baldy. Jack's Creek Trail merges here with Skyline Trail #251, which heads west past the Baldy Peaks to Horsethief Meadow and northeast to Trailrider's Wall and the Santa Barbara Divide.

View to Pecos Baldy from Round Mountain

86

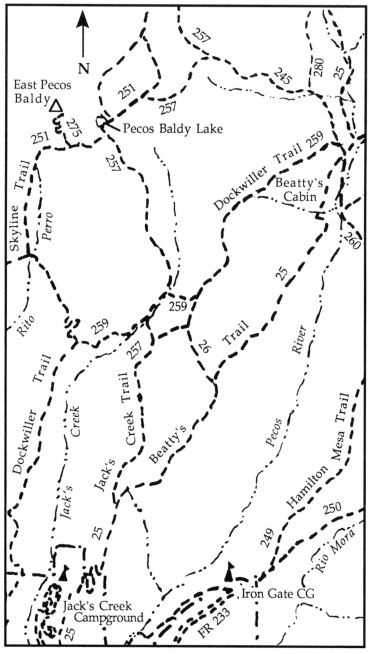

JACK'S CREEK TRAIL #257 (Jack's Creek Campground to Pecos Baldy Lake)

TRAIL #261, #251 (Winsor Creek Campground to Stewart Lake and Horsethief Meadow):
8 miles Moderate Elevation: 8,300-9,800 feet

Although Trail #261 out of Winsor Creek Campground is the quickest route to the Stewart Lake area and is used in place of the actual Winsor Trail #254, the Forest Service has deleted it from its maintenance schedule and encourages hikers to use Winsor Trail instead, which intersects #261 at lower and upper junctions. Trail #251 continues past Stewart Lake to Lake Johnson (Trail #267) and on to Horsethief Meadow.

Winsor Creek Trail #261 follows Winsor Creek up the canyon through lush vegetation of cow parsnip, monkshood, and aspen. The trail crosses to the west side of the creek not far up the trail and continues gradually uphill for about 1 mile until it climbs out of the canyon along the ridge above the creek. You'll pass the lower junction of Winsor Trail, to the left, which is not well defined and easy to miss.

The climb steepens as the trail ascends the ridge, with views over your shoulder to Hamilton Mesa. As the trail reaches the head of the canyon, the upper Winsor Trail junction takes off to the left, and Trail #261 starts to level out. About .25 miles later you'll recross the creek where Trail #251 turns west (left,uphill) to Lake Katherine (this is also the route to Spirit Lake, the continuation of Winsor Trail #254). Follow Trail #251 north (right) along a fairly level route to Stewart Lake, about .5 miles. Signs indicate that there is no camping within the lake basin (meaning on any of the slopes that drain into the lake or its tributaries). The lake is a popular one, and camping sites are available across the trail, away from the basin. Horsethief Meadow is 4.5 miles from Stewart.

Trail #251 continues past the lake where it meanders around a huge swamp area filled with beautiful native grass. A little further on is the junction with Winsor Ridge Trail #271, which leads east 6 miles back down to Cowles.

Trail #251 continues along a fairly level route, with views extending north to the Santa Barbara Divide and the Truchas Peaks. About 1.5 miles past the junction with #271, you'll cross the run-off stream from Johnson Lake; keep a sharp eye out to the west (left), and you'll find the trailhead, usually marked by only a cairn. Johnson Lake, one of the lesser used Pecos Lakes, lies about 2 miles up this trail, a steady climb to the lake basin below Redondo Peak. Camping here is also restricted.

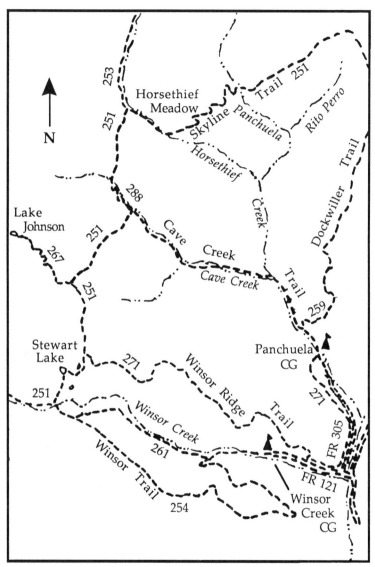

TRAIL #261, #251 (Winsor Creek Campground to
Stewart Lake)

To continue to Horsethief Meadow, stay on Trail #251 as it descends to the Cave Creek basin, about 2 miles down the canyon to the junction with Cave Creek Trail #288 to Panchuela Campground and the continuation of Trail #251 to Horsethief Meadow. Cross Cave Creek and turn northwest (left). It's an easy uphill climb for about .5 miles to where the trail steepens. But the trail quickly levels out through beautiful little meadows filled with sunflowers and *sebadillosos* (skunk cabbage) until it begins the descent to Horsethief Meadow. The last time I visited the meadow, as I came out of the trees into the huge, lush meadows along Horsethief Creek, I immediately saw horses and convinced myself that someone must be reenacting the enterprise that originally named the area—hiding rustled horses in this remote Pecos meadow. But alas, the horses turned out to be tethered and the property of a bunch of *caballeros* from Chimayo.

The meadows here extend for almost 1 mile along the creek and are filled with elephant head, marsh marigold, and tall, lush grass. Trail #251 turns east and climbs 6 miles to Pecos Baldy; Trail #253 heads west toward Panchuela West.

CAVE CREEK TRAIL #288, #251 (Panchuela Campground to Horsethief Meadow):
5 miles   Moderate   Elevation: 8,400-9,800 feet

This is a popular route out of Panchuela Campground and an easy hike to the caves that name the trail. The hike from the caves to Horsethief Meadow junction is quite strenuous and less used.

Cross the footbridge to the north side of Panchuela Creek, and head northwest along the ridge above the creek. The trail descends to the creek just north of the campground and continues along fairly level terrain to the junction with Dockwiller Trail #259, which leads north (right) to the Pecos Baldy area. Stay on Trail #288 along the creek until you reach the confluence of Cave and Panchuela Creeks, where the trail crosses Panchuela Creek and follows Cave Creek west (left). The caves lie about .25 miles up the trail where the creek flows underground—a large camping area marks the caves site. The water rushes in and out of the caves, which actually extend quite a distance underground, and travertine formations are all along the face of the caves.

Cave Creek Trail begins a long ascent up the canyon, through lush growth of cow parsnip, wild geranium, nodding onion, and

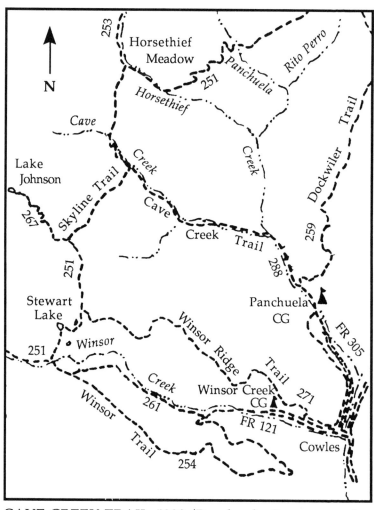

CAVE CREEK TRAIL #228 (Panchuela Campground to Horsethief Meadow)

lousewort. It periodically levels out, but only gets steeper as you near the junction with Trail #251. The last section of trail climbs steeply through a rocky area to where the creek flows next to the trail; Trail #251 heads north to Horsethief Meadow (described in the previous section) and west to Stewart Lake (across Cave Creek).

Pecos Baldy

SKYLINE TRAIL #251 (Horsethief Meadow to Pecos Baldy Lake):
5 miles   Difficult   Elevation: 10,200-11,400 feet

This is one of the more difficult sections of Skyline Trail, but is less traveled and takes you through some spectacular scenery. You can make a base camp in Horsethief Meadow and make this a day hike to avoid carrying a pack up the passes. From the junction of Trail #251 and Trail #253 (the trail to Panchuela West), cross Horsethief Creek and follow it north through the beautiful meadows where the stolen horses used to roam. The meadows continue for about 1 mile, but watch for Trail #251 to start climbing through the trees, away from the creek, at about .5 miles from the junction. The trail climbs up to the top of the pass above the canyon, where it descends down into the Panchuela Creek drainage.

Another 1.5 mile climb brings you to the junction with Trail #256, which crosses the Rito Perro and ties in with Dockwiller Trail #259. Turn north to continue on Trail #251 as it ascends the

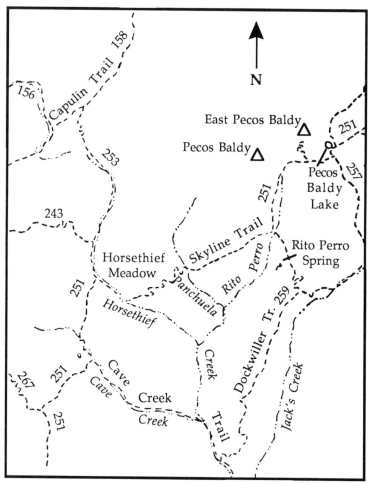

SKYLINE TRAIL #251 (Horsethief Meadow to Pecos
Baldy Lake)

Pecos Baldy ridge in a steep climb to the 12,500-foot mountain.
Trail #275, which leads to the top of the peaks, is passed before
Skyline Trail descends the north side of the peaks to Pecos Baldy
Lake, where the herd of Rocky Mountain bighorn sheep awaits
your arrival, ready for any handouts or deserted packs.

DOCKWILLER TRAIL #259 (Panchuela Campground to Beatty's Flats):
9 miles Difficult Elevation: 8,300-9,400 feet

This trail out of Panchuela Campground leads to the Beatty's Flats area as well as to the Pecos Baldy area, via Trail #256. It's a steeper route to Beatty's than the trails out of Jack's Creek Campground or via Hamilton Mesa, but it takes you quickly into the high country and is replete with scenic views and beautiful alpine vegetation.

To reach the trailhead, take Cave Creek Trail #288 west out of Panchuela Campground (across the bridge at the north end of the area) about .5 miles along Cave Creek to the junction with Trail #259. Dockwiller Trail turns north here and immediately begins to climb along several switchbacks to the top of Mystery Ridge. The switchbacks become steeper as you climb along the east side of the ridge above Jack's Creek.

The trail becomes less steep as it traverses through meadows affording views south from where you have come. The junction with Rito Perro Trail #256, which turns northwest for 1.5 miles to the junction with Skyline Trail #251 (which leads to Pecos Baldy), lies in a large meadow.

Trail #259 turns east through Jack's Creek drainage for about 1 mile until it crosses Jack's Creek. Several spur trails to camping sites may confuse you, but once you reach Trail #257, which basically travels north-south along the creek (to Pecos Baldy Lake or Jack's Creek Campground), follow this trail for about .25 miles until you see a trail that leads across the creek to the right (east) through a small meadow (usually with a fire ring). This is the continuation of Dockwiller Trail to Beatty's.

Trail #259 heads east up the ridge between Jack's Creek and Beatty's Flats. It quickly reaches the top of the ridge and descends several miles into the open meadows above Beatty's Flats (full of *sebadillosos*) where it meets Sebadillosos Trail #245. The Pecos River is just below the trail to the east; Trail #245 climbs the ridge to Trailrider's Wall.

94

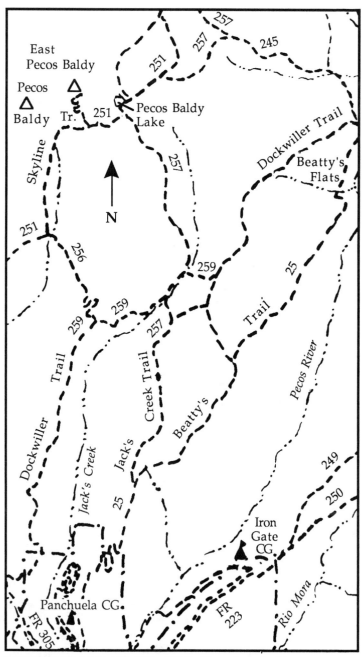

DOCKWILLER TRAIL #259 (Panchuela Campground to Beatty's Flats)

Peñasco Access

The northernmost access to the Pecos, the village of Peñasco, lies beneath the Jicarita and Truchas Peaks of the wilderness high country. The contrast of the green valleys and llanos of this remote, traditional community provides one of the most picturesque scenes in all of northern New Mexico, yet remains a testimony to a very real and important way of life that stresses self-sufficiency and simplicity. Santa Barbara Campground, 4 miles at the end of FR 116 off SH 73 in Peñasco, provides access to the Carson National Forest administered north end of the wilderness, where the West, East, and Middle Fork Santa Barbara trails provide access to the Santa Barbara Divide and Truchas Peaks.

WEST FORK SANTA BARBARA TRAIL #25, #251 (Santa Barbara Campground to Truchas Lakes):
12 miles   Moderate   Elevation: 8,800-12,000 feet

There are some friendly folks in the Pecos Wilderness. The first time we hiked to the Truchas Lakes, two young men from Cordova supplied us with a dinner of fresh trout, caught in the Rio Santa Barbara, and fresh corn, from their mother's garden. Then on the way back to camp, a group of *caballeros* from Ranchos de Taos gave us beer for cocktail hour. Truchas Lakes is a popular destination for the high mountain villagers of the Peñasco area, and the access from Santa Barbara Canyon is fairly easy. Instead of catching the trail that begins right across the road from the wilderness parking area, walk through the campground on the upper loop to the trail that begins next to the river, for a less uphill hike (the two trails meet only a little ways into the hike).

The trail follows the west side of the river in an easy climb through aspen forests. Gooseberry, raspberry and strawberry proliferate along the trail; views of the high Pecos peaks are visible almost immediately. A sign about 1 mile up indicates that this is West Fork Trail #25, with distances of 10 miles to the Santa Barbara Divide (the north-south ridge that separates the two watersheds of the Pecos) and 14 miles to Pecos Falls (via Middle Fork Trail).

About .5 miles farther up the canyon, the trail crosses the river and continues to climb to the junction of the West and Middle Fork Trails, at about 2 miles up. The sign says Pecos Falls to your

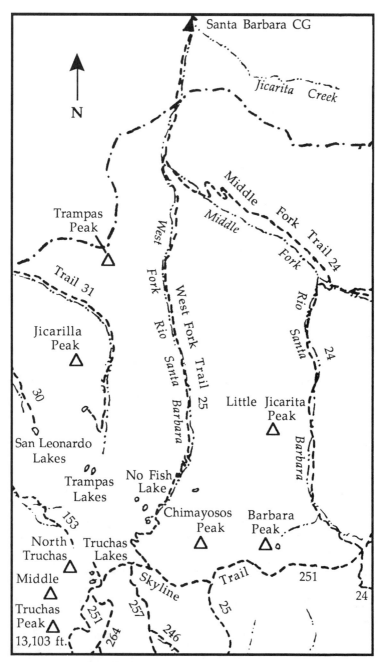

WEST FORK TRAIL #25, #251 (Santa Barbara Campground to Truchas Lakes)

left (east) along Middle Fork Trail #24, and the Santa Barbara Divide and Truchas Lakes straight ahead on West Fork Trail #25. Follow Trail #25 as it traverses a small meadow, then crosses the middle fork of the Rio Santa Barbara (the west fork of the river is still on your right).

The trail soon begins its long, gentle ascent through the meadows that dominate the terrain, full of tulip gentians, *sebadillosos*, and cinquefoil. Aspens line the canyon walls, the sounds of the river accompany you on your walk, and Chimayosos Peak looms ahead, marking the divide.

After several miles of meadow, the trail crosses the Rio Santa Barbara to the west side of the canyon, where a sign indicates it's 6 miles to the divide (you have to look around for a river crossing here, as there is no bridge or natural crossing right along the trail). Trail #25 begins a somewhat steeper climb along the side of the canyon in the spruce-fir forest as it leaves the river in the canyon bottom. A series of switchbacks crosses several river tributaries, one of which descends from No Fish Lake, which lies just to the right of the trail after the switchbacks temporarily straighten out (the lake is so named because it freezes during the winter and can't support a fish population). Keep a sharp eye out for the hidden lake, down from the trail just a few hundred yards. There are a few campsites near here, and as with all the Pecos Lakes, it is best not to camp in the lake basin.

At tree line the trail turns southeast and switchbacks up the scree slopes in a moderate climb to the divide. Alpine vegetation grows low to the ground. You can see the northernmost of the peaks in the Truchas formation over your shoulder; keep an eye out for the herd of Rocky Mountain bighorn sheep that lives in this rocky terrain between here and Truchas Lakes.

At the top of the divide, you are truly in the heart of the Pecos. Stretched out before you is the Pecos watershed, with miles and miles of wilderness descending to Cowles and the Santa Fe Ski Basin. Hamilton Mesa is immediately visible, with its huge, open meadows of chartreuse green breaking the monotony of the deep forest green. Looking back where you have been you will see the Rio Santa Barbara Valley stretching north to the wilderness boundary, defined by Jicarita Peak. A spur trail leads off to the right toward North Truchas Peak (the other Truchas Peaks are still hidden by a small ridge in front of you). Trail #25 terminates here with Skyline Trail #251. To the left, Trail #251 heads across the slopes of Chimayosos Peak toward the junction with Middle Fork

Rocky Mountain Bighorn Sheep at the Truchas Lakes

Trail #24 and on east across the divide. Skyline Trail west continues about 1 mile to the Truchas Lakes, your destination.

Follow Trail #251 south (straight ahead) down off the divide, where it descends a ridge into mixed conifer forest and small meadows as it bears southwest to the lakes. Not far down the trail you come around the ridge, and there, before you, stand the three Truchas Peaks, and further south, East Pecos Baldy and Pecos Baldy. Unless you go ahead and climb Truchas Peak at 13,103 feet, you can't get much higher than this in the Pecos Wilderness.

An alternate route that ties in with Trail #251 heading east across the divide turns off to the left near some campsites and flowing springs (look for the yellow monkeyflower on the creek banks). Stay on #251 west about .25 miles, follow the trail as it turns to the right, and climb a short distance to the lakes. Middle Truchas Peak sits right there above you as you emerge into the lower lake basin. The higher lake sits just above this first lake and can be easily reached by the trail around the north side of the lake. If you follow the main trail around to the south side of the lake, access trails up Truchas Peak start out of the meadow beside the lake. Again, there should be no camping in the lake basin, to protect the fragile shoreline vegetation and prevent pollution of the waters. If you sit quietly by the lake, sooner or later some of the bighorn sheep herd will show up to see what good things you have to eat.

From Truchas Lakes, Skyline Trail continues south, down out of the lake basin (watch for the trail as it dips down to the right, away from the campsite area), across several scree fields where you are very likely to see (and hear—the campers from Cordova called it a "whistler") the little pika, a rabbit-related creature that lives in this high mountain terrain. Another small lake lies just across a scree field, and Skyline Trail meets Trail #264 (which heads south towards Beatty's Flats) just beyond that. Skyline Trail continues south along Trailrider's Wall to East Pecos Baldy.

MIDDLE FORK SANTA BARBARA TRAIL #24 (Santa Barbara Campground to Santa Barbara Divide):
12 miles   Moderate   Elevation: 8,800-12,000 feet

Another northside route out of the town of Peñasco, Middle Fork Santa Barbara also leads to the Santa Barbara Divide (along with West Fork and East Fork) and is the quickest route from the north to Pecos Falls. The trailhead is at the east end of Santa Barbara Campground (see previous section) and accesses all three trails—West, Middle and East Forks.

At the 2-mile mark, Middle Fork Trail #24 separates from West Fork Trail and begins to climb the canyon to the east, high above Middle Fork Rio Santa Barbara. The trail stays up on the ridge for about 2 miles before it meets the river in a large meadow. Just beyond where the East and Middle Forks of the river divide, the trail also divides: East Fork River Trail #26 continues southeast along the East Fork Rio Santa Barbara to the divide; Middle Fork Trail #24 crosses East Fork Rio Santa Barbara and follows it back downstream about .25 miles to Middle Fork Rio Santa Barbara where it turns south to follow the river. Trail #24 follows the east side of the river canyon for about 1 mile, then crosses to the west side. Numerous crossings of tributaries make it a wet hike, similar to the West Fork Trail. The trail crosses a tributary from a small lake below Santa Barbara Peak just below the divide; here the trail divides—both trails lead to the top of the divide and terminate at the junction with trails #251, Skyline Trail, and Trail #24, which leads south to Pecos Falls.

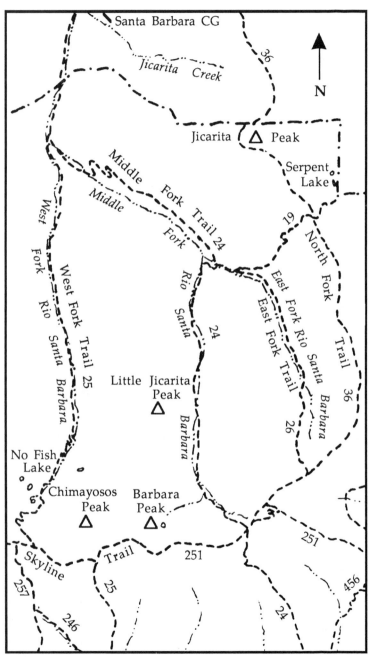

MIDDLE FORK SANTA BARBARA TRAIL #24;
EAST FORK SANTA BARBARA TRAIL #26

EAST FORK SANTA BARBARA #26 (Santa Barbara Campground
to Santa Barbara Divide):
12 miles   Moderate   Elevation: 8,800-12,000 feet

This is the least used of the three trails leading to the Santa
Barbara Divide from Santa Barbara Campground and is hard to
follow near the base of the divide. To access the trail, take Middle
Fork Trail #24 south at the east end of the campground (see
description in West Fork Santa Barbara section).

At the 2-mile mark, Middle Fork Trail #24 separates from West
Fork Trail and begins to climb the canyon to the east, high above
Middle Fork Rio Santa Barbara. The trail stays up on the ridge for
about 2 miles before it meets the river in a large meadow. Just
beyond where the East and Middle Forks of the river divide, the
trail also divides: East Fork River Trail #26 continues southeast
along the East Fork Rio Santa Barbara to the divide; Middle Fork
Trail #24 crosses East Fork Rio Santa Barbara and follows it back
downstream about .25 miles to Middle Fork Rio Santa Barbara
where it turns south to follow the river.

Follow East Fork Trail #26 east along the river through open
meadows. At about .25 miles it meets Agua Piedra Trail #19
descending from Jicarita Peak ridge. Trail #26 gradually swings to
the south as it enters a canyon between Jicarita Peak ridge and
another ridge to the west descending from the divide. East Fork
Trail parallels Trail #36, which follows Jicarita Peak Ridge from
the Divide north to Ripley Point.

Trail #26 follows East Fork Rio Santa Barbara through meadows interspersed with mixed conifer and aspen forests. Numerous tributaries of the East Fork plunge down the sides of the
canyon farther up the trail to the base of the divide, where the
canyon levels out and the trail becomes less discernible as it traverses a series of marshy areas. Follow the various tree blazes and
cairns that mark the way.

The trail reaches the top of the divide east of Santa Barbara
Peak, overlooking what is called the Rincon Bonito to the south,
and meets Trail #36. To the east Trail #36 follows the divide along
Jicarita Peak ridge to Ripley Point and west up the ridge to Skyline Trail #251.

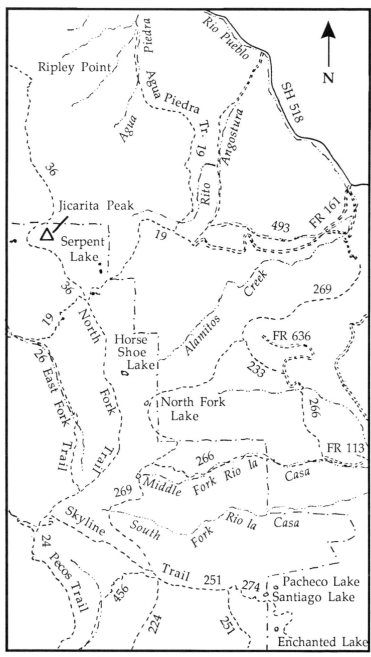

AGUA PIEDRA TRAIL #19 (FR 161 to North Fork
Trail)

AGUA PIEDRA TRAIL #19 (FR 161 to Trail #36):
4 miles   Moderate   Elevation: 10,200-12,400 feet

This trail provides a quicker route to the Santa Barbara Divide than the trails accessed from Santa Barbara Campground. Trail #19 actually originates in Agua Piedra Campground outside the wilderness boundary, but can be accessed by a forest road and spur trail to get you closer to the wilderness. To find the trailhead, take SH 75 north out of Peñasco towards Taos and the junction with SH 518. Turn east and follow SH 518 past Agua Piedra Campground and the town of Tres Ritos 13.7 miles to FR 161, before Holman Hill. Turn right onto the forest road and follow this all-weather road 4.4 miles to its termination at the spur trailhead parking lot.

About .5 miles from this trailhead is where Trail #19 ascends from Agua Piedra Campground 7 miles to the north (much of the the trail to the campground is actually a primitive road). Follow the continuation of Trail #19 to the west (left) as it climbs 3 miles toward Serpent Lake. At .75 miles the trail crosses the irrigation ditch to Holman, New Mexico, then continues in a steady uphill climb to the switchbacks across the small meadows that define the terrain. Here you will find the brisltlecone pines, some of the oldest trees growing in the Pecos. The climb to the wilderness boundary, at about 2.5 miles, is fairly gradual, with occasional steep places.

A sign marks the spur trail leading down to Serpent Lake to the north (right) after about .5 miles. A short, steep trail takes you down to the lake (actually two small lakes) basin in its spectacular setting below the Jicarita Peak ridge. Gentians, rose crown, and elephant head fill the basin meadows.

Back on Trail #19, a moderate climb reveals views of the lake below, as well as east towards Mora and north to Taos. At tree line, switchbacks continue to the top of the Jicarita Peak ridge that extends to Santa Barbara Divide. Here, North Fork Trail #36 heads south along the ridge to Skyline Trail and north around Jicarita Peak to Ripley Point. The view is spectacular: northwest over the three forks of the Santa Barbara River loom Chimayosos Peak, the Truchas Peaks, Sheep's Head, and Trampas Peak.

Trail #19 contines west down a steep ascent (from 12,400 feet to just over 10,000 feet) to the junction of East Fork Santa Barbara Trail #26, which leads south to the divide and north to Santa Barabara Campground.

TRAIL #30 (San Leonardo Lakes):
3.5 miles   Moderate   Elevation: 9,000-11,400 feet

This trail to San Leonardo Lakes leads to the high country in a moderate climb through dense Englemann spruce forest and can be used as access to Jicarilla Peak and San Leonardo Peak. To find the trailhead, take SH 76 south out of Peñasco 4.6 miles to FR 207. Follow this road east through the beautiful village of El Valle for 7.9 miles to FR 639, which turns south (right). Driving this road requires a high clearance vehicle to negotiate the low spots and a four-wheel drive in rainy weather to negotiate the mud. Cross the Rio de las Trampas and follow FR 639 1.4 miles to the sign which indicates the turn to Trail #30; turn left, and the trailhead is about .4 miles up the road.

The trail immediately enters dense stands of spruce as it ascends this narrow canyon alongside the Rio San Leonardo. The first part of the hike is a gradual ascent; monkshood and thimbleberry grow profusely under the spruce canopy. There are numerous river crossings but rocks and logs provide easy access.

About two-thirds of the way up, the trail steepens, then levels out in an open area where numerous campsites are available. Past the headwaters of the river, the trail steepens again, and visible are views of the Jicarilla Peak ridge which separates this canyon from Trampas Canyon where Trail #31 climbs to the Trampas Lakes.

The trail levels out again, skirts the first lake, and terminates at the second, larger lake which sits in a cirque below Leonardo Peak, visible on the ridge to the east, and Jicarilla Peak, just to the northeast. The water in the lakes is almost black, perhaps due to tremendous tree-fall from the steep canyon walls. We've found snow on the north facing slope in September. Fire rings are scattered around the lakes, but be sure to camp away from the basin to prevent polluting the area.

You can climb from the lakes up to the ridge and access Jicarilla Peak or climb down into Trampas Canyon to Trail #31.

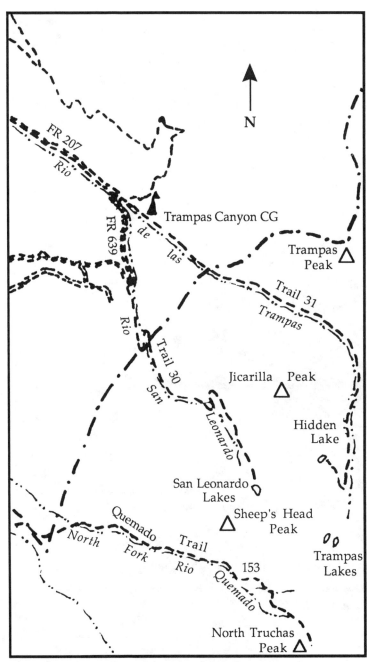

SAN LEONARDO TRAIL #30

San Leorardo Lake

Española Access

Many of the trails that access the Pecos from the west side near Española provide long routes to the heart of the high country, but tend to be used less than the Pecos or Santa Fe Ski Basin sides. You're also apt to run into a lot of *caballeros* from the local villages riding their horses to avoid the long hikes. Borrego Mesa, on FR 306 off SH 4, offers several routes into the Horsethief Meadow and Pecos Baldy area as well as to the Truchas Peaks.

RIO MEDIO TRAIL #155 (Borrego Campground to Trailrider's Wall):
10 miles   Moderate   Elevation: 8,600-11,600 feet

This is a three-shoe hike: boots for the trail, thongs for the river crossings, and dry sneakers for camp. The route follows the Rio Medio most of the way; unfortunately, the river has washed away numerous sections of the trail, necessitating bushwacking and unweildy crossings. But it's a lovely hike, replete with lush wild-flowers and grasses. Fewer people use this west side of the Pecos, and you may well hike this trail in complete solitude.

To find the trailhead at Borrego Mesa Campground, take SH 4 at Pojoaque and continue through Nambe to the village of Cundiyo. Several miles north of the village (just beyond the turn-off to Santa Cruz Lake) FR 306 (an all-weather road) heads east, leading 9 miles to FR 435, which turns right into the campground. The Rio Medio trailhead is on the spur road just to the right of the campground entrance. A sign indicates that it's 5 miles to Rio Capulin Trail and 10 miles to Trailrider's Wall.

Trail #155 heads .5 miles down into Rio Medio Canyon. Once along the river, it ascends in a gentle climb on the north side through thick undergrowth of skyrocket gilia, geranium, cow parsnip (the big white flowers along the river banks), monarda (wild oregano), and thimbleberry. You'll soon come to the first section of trail washed out by the river, and you'll have to cross to the south side, then quickly cross back to the north. There are few places where logs or rocks provide dry crossings, so be ready to don your thongs.

The trail soon climbs farther up the north side of the canyon skirting several creek drainages that flow into the river below. The climb steepens as the trail enters an aspen grove, then descends

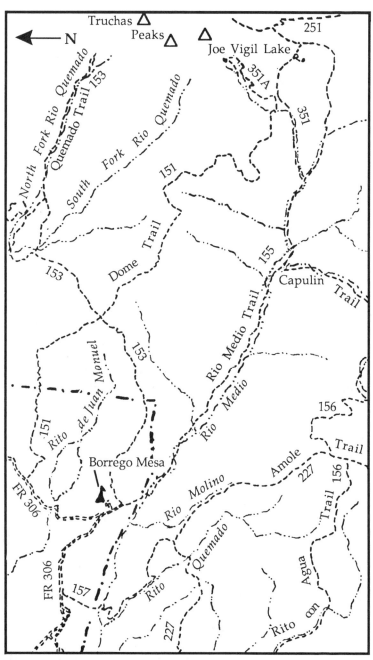

RIO MEDIO TRAIL #155

again to the river. Several more washouts require river crossings, and the trail ends up on the south side. At the 5-mile mark you enter a horse corral (a beautifully constructed log fence), and an old, broken-up trail sign on the ground indicates the junction with Rio Capulin Trail #158, which climbs south out of the Rio Medio drainage. You can just make out the print on the sign that indicates that the trail continues to Brazos Cabin just ahead and on to Pecos Baldy Lake. Continue east on Trail #155 through a grotto-like area and back out of the corral until another river crossing—the river is less wide here and the crossings are easier—brings you to a beautiful meadow, site of the old Brazos cabin. Here a tributary of the Rio Medio flows into the river from the southeast, while the main river branch continues northeast up the canyon. Views from the meadow extend east to the backside of Pecos Baldy. It's an obvious campsite, although just ahead on the trail several other sites farther off the trail provide more privacy.

Trail #155 follows the river in a gentle climb through fields of thimbleberry, blue and white columbine, and monkey flower. The trail crosses the river several times, but logs provide easy access. At 1.5 miles from the meadow is the turn north to Joe Vigil Lake, Trail #351, at an obvious campsite. Trail #351 is a hard-to-follow trail that leads to the spur trail #351A, which accesses the little used lake (Trail #351 continues to several smaller lakes and ties in with Trail #155 at Trailrider's Wall).

Follow the south fork of Rio Medio on Trail #155 as it continues to cross the stream back and forth from north to south. At the head of the canyon, the trail disappears in a boggy meadow of *sebadillos*. To find the route, cross the meadow to the north side and look for the trail heading up the east slope. The trail then turns west, and when you reach the top of the ridge, you can see the two small lakes accessed by Trail #351. You will be on the northeast side of these lakes as the trail climbs northwest up the side of Trailrider's Wall and meets Skyline Trail #251, which heads north to the Truchas Peaks and south to Pecos Baldy Lake. You're in the high country now, at 11,600 feet, with a great view from Trailrider's Wall extending west.

CAPULIN TRAIL #158, #150 (Trail #155 to Aspen Ranch):
12 miles Moderate Elevtation: 9,400-10,000 feet

This hike can be accessed from either Borrego Mesa Campground via Trail #155 or from Borrego Trail #150 at Aspen Ranch near the Santa Fe Ski Basin. Either way you will encounter up and down terrain as you pass through various river drainages and the beautiful alpine meadows of Panchuela West.

The access from the west side at Borrego Mesa Campground (directions to the campground are given in the previously described hike) follow Rio Medio Trail #155 5 miles east to the junction with Rio Capulin Trail #158 in the horse corral. Trail #158 ascends along a creek drainage 2 miles to the junction with Trail #253. The climb is moderate, through lush vegetation of bluebell, shooting star, and thimbleberry. The trail reminds me of the rain forests of the northwest it is so wet and thick with wildflowers and undergrowth. The trail stays primarily on the west side of the creek, although crosses the creek several times at various washouts.

Trail #253 branches east 6 miles to Horsethief Meadow; Trail #158 continues southwest in a .5-mile steeper climb to the top of the ridge. Here it levels out and soon passes the little used Trail #156, which heads west back to Borrego Mesa. Trail #158 begins its descent into the Rio Frijoles basin and soon crosses the headwaters of the Rio Frijoles and once again becomes wet and lush. The trail stays on the west side of the river down through boggy meadows full of elephant head, the strange looking spike plant with pink flowers that look like elephant trunks. The trail follows the river more closely as it passes through a fence into the area called Panchuela West, a series of river meadows full of wildflowers and grazing cattle. A spur trail leads west to the Forest Service administrative cabin, an old stone and wood structure that is in a state of disrepair.

Trail #158 continues south along the river and soon passes the junction of Trail #243, which leads east to Horsethief Meadow. Several river crossings wind through fields of cinquefoil, the beautiful, lavendar sky pilot, and yarrow. The river widens as you descend through the meadows, and crossings become more of a problem. The trail then becomes a three-shoe hike just like Rio Medio Trail—you'll need thongs or sneakers to get you across the river. After several crossings the trail continues on the east side to a fence. This is where Trail #158 leaves the Rio Frijoles and climbs

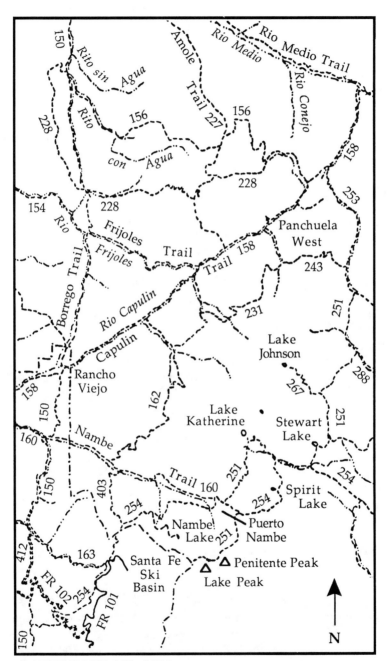

CAPULIN TRAIL #158

the ridge to the east to the Rio Capulin drainage. Watch for the hard to see trail as it veers away from the Rio Frijoles just before the fence, crosses the river, and begins to climb the ridge. There is a trail sign on the other side of the fence that indicates the continuation of Trail #154 to Cundiyo along the Rio Frijoles and the turn to Rancho Viejo along Rio Capulin Trail.

A .5-mile climb brings you to the top of the ridge, where the trail then switchbacks down to the headwaters of the Rio Capulin. There are few campsites along this portion of the trail, until you reach the junction with Capulin Cienega Trail #162, which leads southeast to the Rio Nambe. A clearing provides a lovely campsite, where I've watched deer browse in the early morning (a signless post marks the junction).

A gradual 2-mile descent along the west side of the Rio Capulin brings you to the wilderness boundary sign, which marks the beginning of the pivate land of Rancho Viejo, a meadow area used for grazing. Several trails meet here as the route leaves Rio Capulin Trail and follows Borrego Trail #150 to Aspen Ranch. Cross the Rio Capulin; a sign indicates the continuation of Trail #158 southwest along the river to the Rio Nambe. Borrego Trail #150 north crosses back over the Rio Capulin and heads towards Borrego Mesa. Borrego Trail #150 south, leads 1.5 miles to the Rio Nambe. The sign here also says it is 7 miles back to Panchuela West where you just came from, and 12 miles to Brazos Cabin, which I think is inaccurate, as the entire Rio Capulin Trail is 10 miles.

Follow Borrego Trail #150 as it climbs the ridge to the east above the meadows of Rancho Viejo. The climb is fairly steep through drier ponderosa pine country, with several campsites available. The trail then drops over into the Rio Nambe drainage and switchbacks down to the river, where it meets Rio Nambe Trail #160, heading east 6 miles to Puerto Nambe. A heavily used campsite by the river indicates the proximity to civilization—it's only 2 miles to Aspen Ranch from here.

Cross the log bridge over Rio Nambe Trail #160, which heads west and follows the river to its trailhead. Trail #150 begins a gentle climb along a small drainage—the terrain is again wet and lush—as it ascends to Aspen Ranch. The bright purple monkshood grows all along the trail. The terrain is steeper and hotter the second mile to where the trail emerges on FR 412, .5 miles from Aspen Ranch. A parking pull-off and powerline mark the spot, as there is no trail sign. FR 412 continues south .5 miles to the meadows of Aspen Ranch, then continues across the creek to the right for another 2 miles to FR 102. Turn left on FR 102 and continue 3 miles to the Santa Fe Ski Basin Road 475, which leads 12 miles to Santa Fe.

Section IV. San Pedro Parks

San Pedro Parks Wilderness is aptly named. Although the wilderness is at an elevation of 10,000 feet, no rugged peaks rise up above the trail; no steep canyons descend to the abyss. Instead, miles and miles of trail meander through wet mountain meadows—parks—alongside quiet creeks of cutthroat trout. Thick aspen groves provide sheltered campsites; dark green spruce and fir create a feeling of mountain serenity and isolation. After a rain, the wide, gentle trails turn to mud, the creeks jump their banks, and the meadows sparkle with dew-drop jewels. It is a world foreign to our semi-arid sensibility, and I'm sure it's good for us.

San Pedro Parks is really the San Pedro Mountains north of the Jemez Mountains in Santa Fe National Forest. Many of the trails lead to what is called "the Parks," the central meadowlands of this 41,132-acre wilderness, established in 1965. Here, small trout ponds dot the huge landscape of the wide open plateau filled with native grasses and alpine gentians, under a canopy of expansive blue sky. This wilderness does not see the intense use of the Pecos and Wheeler Peak areas. Many of those familiar with the wilderness are local people of Cuba, Regina, Coyote, and Gallina. During hunting season, these folks, long accustomed to the taste of venison and elk, stalk the Parks on foot and horseback, searching for the large herds that roam the meadows. San Gregorio Reservoir, at the southern entrance to the Parks, is a popular fishing spot and was established as an irrigation source before the wilderness designation. Access to the San Pedro Parks Wilderness is from the town of Cuba, via SH 126 and FR 70, and various forest roads off SH 96 through Gallina and Regina.

VACAS TRAIL #51:
9 miles   Moderate   Elevation: 9,300-10,382 feet

Vacas Trail is the main artery of the San Pedro Parks Wilderness trail system and ties into a network of trails that crisscross the wilderness. To reach the trailhead take SH 126 east from the town of Cuba 12 miles to FR 70. This forest access road leads north 2.7 miles to a parking area at the wilderness boundary (the road continues around the wilderness to several other trailheads as well).

The short, 1-mile trip to San Gregorio Reservoir is along a gentle, canopied path. The Forest Service has prohibited camping near the reservoir to preserve the fragile shoreline, but you'll undoubtedly see a lot of day-use fishing here before you escape further into the wilderness.

In the reservoir meadow follow Vacas Trail along the eastern edge, in the trees. Another trail continues north across the meadow and ties in with the main Vacas Trail at the north end of the reservoir, where a sign states that camping and open fires are prohibited. Here the trail heads northeast up an easy incline to Clear Creek. Cross the stream to the east side, and follow the creek north in a gentle ascent. About 1 mile later the creek forks; Vacas Trail continues to the right through an alpine meadow ringed with spruce, fir and aspen. At the north end of the meadow the trail crosses the creek again and heads north into the trees.

From here to the Palomas Trail junction, Vacas Trail winds its way north across several ridges and through beautiful alpine meadows to the Rio de las Vacas. The trail crosses the river to the east side, where a sign marks the junction with Palomas Trail #50, which heads southeast 3.8 miles to FR 70.

Vacas Trail continues north along the river valley for several hundred yards, where it recrosses the creek and meets Anastacio Trail #435, a 3.3-mile trail west that connects Vacas Trail and Los Pinos Trail #46, which originates on FR 95, also out of Cuba.

Vacas Trail follows the wide river valley in an easy 2.4-mile walk to the junction with Peñas Negras Trail #32, which leads to the southeast corner of the wilderness. At this junction Vacas Trail leaves the Rio de las Vacas and heads northwest to the Parks. The trails crosses several large meadows full of fringed and tulip gentian, bushy cinquefoil, and *sebadillosos*. You'll know you've reached the Parks when its size overwhelms you—a huge meadow of chartreuse green hues ringed by the deep evergreen of

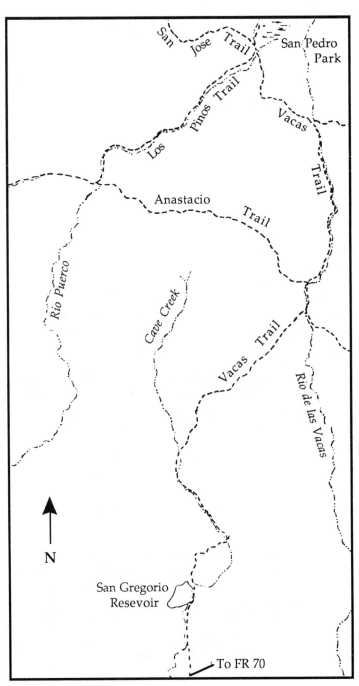

VACAS TRAIL #51

spruce-fir. Small fishing ponds dot the meadow, and an old Forest Service cabin sits on the north side, frequented by local cowboys and occasional hikers.

Los Pinos and San Jose trails meet Vacas Trail on the west side of the meadow. San Jose Trail #33 leads 6.5 miles north to FR 96; Los Pinos Trail #46 leads 2.6 west to Anastacio Trail and on out of the Wilderness to FR 95 (3.3 miles).

PALOMAS TRAIL #50:
3.8 miles   Moderate   Elevation: 9,100-10,200 feet

This is the shortest route to the Parks from FR 70 out of Cuba. The first mile of the trail is steeper than Vacas Trail, but once you reach the top of the plateau the walk is just as easy. The trailhead lies about 8.5 miles on FR 70 from the junction of SH 126. A sign there identifies the trailhead, giving the distance to the Rio de las Vacas, 3 miles (the maps say it's 3.8 miles), 1 mile to the Rito de las Perchas, and 7.25 miles to the Parks.

The first mile is a moderate climb through thick spruce-fir vegetation to a large meadow where views extend northwest to the Jemez Mountains. A short descent from the meadow brings you to the Rito de las Perchas, where Perchas Trail #418 follows the creek northeast 2.3 miles to the junction with Peñas Negras Trail (which in turn leads north to Vacas Trail and south to FR 70) and on to Vega Redonda, where it intersects Rio Puerco Trail #385 (which heads west to Vacas Trail and east to Rio Puerco Campground off SH 96).

Cross the creek and follow it just a short distance to where the trails divides. Turn northwest (left) to follow Palomas Trail through a meadow as it begins a short climb to another meadow where the elevation levels off. Wooden posts mark the way through the sometimes overgrown grasses in the meadows. Just before the junction with Vacas Trail, the trail turns west and meets the Rio de las Vacas as the river heads out of the wilderness. Palomas Trail follows a bend around the river to Vacas Trail, which leads south 4.3 miles to San Gregorio Reservoir and FR 70, and north to San Pedro Parks.

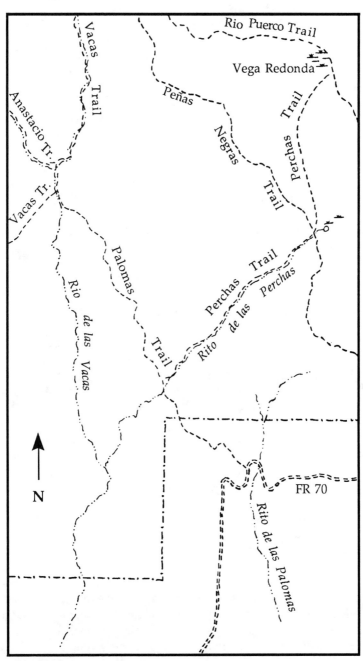

PALOMAS TRAIL #50

ANASTACIO TRAIL #435:
2.6 miles Easy Elevation: 10,200 feet

This trail traverses the wilderness east to west and connects Vacas Trail with Los Pinos Trail. It's an easy hike through typical San Pedro Parks terrain—meadows ringed with spruce-fir forest.

The eastern trailhead is at Vacas Trail, just north of the junction of the Las Palomas-Vacas junction, about 5 miles north of San Gregorio Reservoir. The trail follows the meandering Rito Anastacio through a large meadow until it climbs a small ridge, where it leaves the creek at the "Fish for Fun" sign. The trail continues west through more meadows and boggy areas until it makes a gentle ascent to the junction with Los Pinos Trail #46, where views west over the edge of the wilderness stretch to the mesas beyond Cuba. Los Pinos Trail continues 3.3 miles west to FR 95, and 2.6 miles northeast to the Parks.

LOS PINOS TRAIL #46:
6 miles Moderate-Difficult Elevation: 8,600-10,100 feet

This is a relatively steep route to the Parks, accessed out of Cuba. In town, turn right onto FR 95. At 4.6 miles the road turns right again and travels 3 miles to the trailhead. The last .2 miles require a vehicle with high clearance—you might want to park at about the 2-mile mark, where there is another forest road to the right that provides some parking spots.

Los Pinos Trail follows the canyon bottom in a fairly steep climb (2,000 feet in 3 miles), crossing the Rito de Los Pinos numerous times. The trail climbs through the mixed conifer of the Canadian life zone with periodic stands of aspen coloring the canyon in the fall. On the upper part of the hike, the trail stays on the north side of the canyon, where views out over the red mesas beyond Cuba open up.

At the head of the canyon the trail levels out considerably and intersects Anastacio Trail #435, which turns southeast for 2.6 miles to Vacas Trail. Los Pinos Trail continues northeast through one of the prettiest parts of the wilderness, along the narrow canyon of the Rito de Los Pinos. Just past the trail junction it crosses a large meadow, then ascends the canyon to several beaver ponds, where signs of their feverous activity are evident everywhere.

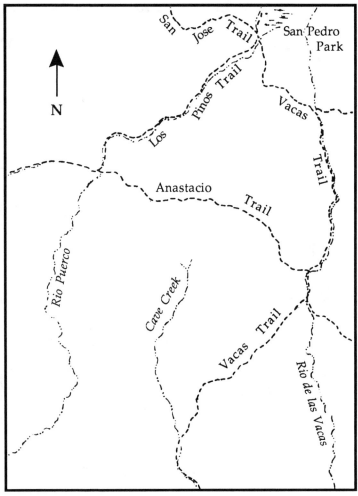

ANASTACIO TRAIL #435

The trail continues gradually uphill through spruce-fir forest and narrow canyon meadows to the Parks, where at the west end of the huge Parks' meadow the trail meets Vacas Trail, heading south, and San Jose Trail #33, which heads north 6.5 miles to FR 96. Los Pinos Trail provides excellent campsites throughout the narrow canyon ascent to the Parks.

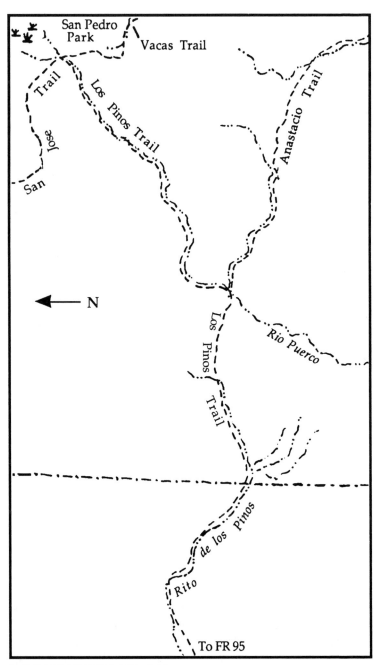

LOS PINOS TRAIL #46

Beaver pond on Los Pinos Trail

PERCHAS TRAIL #418:
4.2 miles   Moderate   Elevation: 9,600-10,000 feet

This is an interior trail that is accessed from Palomas Trail #50 on the south and Rio Puerco Trail #385 (Highline Trail) on the north. The trail follows the Rito de las Perchas through a relatively narrow canyon filled with meadows.

To access the trail from the south end, take FR 70 off SH 126 for 8.5 miles to the Palomas trailhead. Climb Palomas Trail (about 1 mile) to where it descends to the Rito de las Perchas. Las Perchas Trail turns northeast along the river through a stand of spruce-fir and then emerges into the canyon meadows, where it follows the river along a leisurely route. At about the 2-mile mark, the trail becomes less distinguishable, but stays on the west side of the canyon near the trees as it climbs to the ridge where it junctions with Peñas Negras Trail #32. Watch for a rock cairn on top of the ridge marking the route. There should be a sign in the clearing indicating Peñas Negras Trail northwest to the junction with Vacas Trail (3.5 miles) and southeast to the trailhead on FR 70 (3.25 miles).

Perchas Trail continues north from the headwaters of the Rito

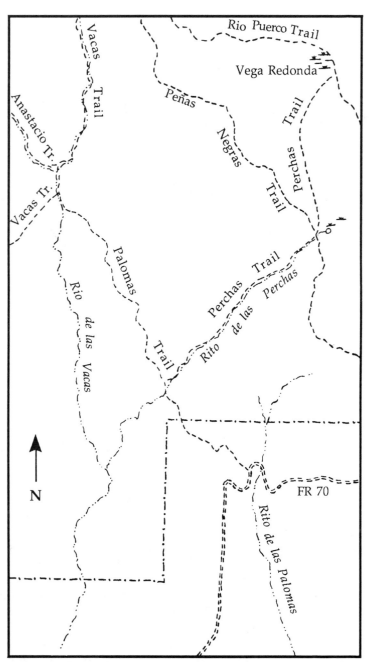

PERCHAS TRAIL #418

de las Perchas another 1.9 miles to the junction with Rio Puerco Trail, at the south end of Vega Redonda, one of the most beautiful of the area's meadows. Rio Puerco Trail continues northwest around the meadow and on to Vacas Trail; to the southeast it heads 3 miles to the trailhead at FR 93 near Rio Puerco Campground.

PEÑAS NEGRAS TRAIL #32:
9 miles   Moderate   Elevation: 9,300-10,300 feet

One of the longest trails in San Pedro Parks, Peñas Negras Trail begins on FR 70 out of Cuba and intersects Rio Puerco Trail about 1.5 miles southeast of the Parks. To reach the trailhead take SH 126 out of Cuba to FR 70 and travel approximately 10 miles to the trailhead.

It's a gentle climb northwest to the junction with Perchas Trail in a large meadow where the trails are not well defined. Look for a large cairn marking Perchas Trail and a sign indicating the continuation of Peñas Negras Trail to the northwest. The trail continues through meadows 2.5 miles to the junction with Rio Puerco Trail, which turns west for about .5 miles to Vacas Trail (the junction with Rio Capulin Trail is passed en route).

SAN JOSE TRAIL #33:
6.5 miles   Moderate   Elevation: 8,600-10,382 feet

San Jose Trail leads to the Parks from the north side of the wilderness and provides a little more of a climb than the trails accessing the Parks from FR 70. To find the trailhead, take SH 96 north from SH 44 (several miles west of Cuba) 8 miles to FR 96. Turn south (right) and follow this dirt road 4.5 miles to the trailhead. The last mile is quite rocky, neccesitating a high clearance vehicle.

The trail climbs the canyon next to the San Jose Creek, through spruce-fir vegetation interspersed with stands of aspen, making this a perfect fall hike. The trail can be quite wet, with numerous creek crossings. At about 1.5 miles, as the trail switchbacks up the canyon, you get a view north out over the towns of Regina and Gallina toward the Jicarilla Apache Indian Reservation. Large stands of aspen cover the canyon hillsides.

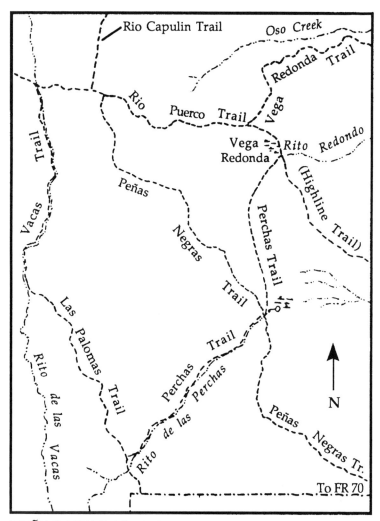

PEÑAS NEGRAS TRAIL #32

At the head of the canyon the trail emerges into a small mead-ow at the headwaters of the creek. It soon reenters the forest and continues to gradually climb toward the Parks, along the San Jose Ridge. Auxiliary canyons tie into the trail as it periodically levels out and enters small meadows. At about the 4-mile mark is the junction with Upper Gallina Trail #36, a 2.6-mile interior trail which connects San Jose Trail with Red Rock Trail #30. San Jose

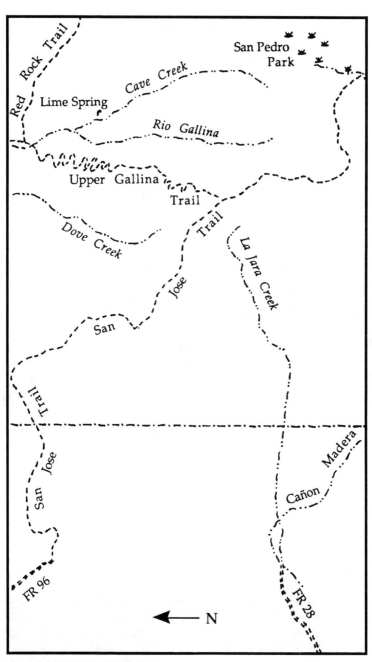

SAN JOSE TRAIL #33

Trail continues another 2 miles through mixed conifer forest and meadow to the Parks, where it junctions at the northwest corner of the meadow with Los Pinos Trail #46, which leads west 6 miles to FR 95, and Vacas Trail #51, which leads 9 miles south past San Gregorio Lake to FR 70.

RIO CAPULIN TRAIL #31:
8 miles   Moderate-Difficult   Elevation: 9,000-10,000 feet

This long, fairly difficult trail ascends to the Parks from the north end off SH 96 and meets Peñas Negras Trail just west of Trail #385. The trail is not well defined once it enters the high park meadows, but cairns and posts do show the way.

To access Rio Capulin Trail take SH 96 northeast past the town of Gallina, where FR 103 turns south 23 miles from the junction with SH 44. Just across the cattle guard, FR 76 turns right (west) and parallels the highway until it turns south again near the junction with FR 171. Turn left onto FR 171 and follow it south to the trailhead, about 1 mile in. The trail begins at Cecelia Springs and climbs quite steeply through spruce-fir vegetation mixed with aspen to the junction with Red Rock Trail #30 at 1.3 miles. The Rio Capulin flows about .25 miles west of the junction. Rio Capulin Trail continues less steeply south along some new sections of trail as it climbs toward the Parks. The trail passes through the highest section of the Parks to the east of the San Pedro Peaks at about 4 miles. Stands of thick spruce intersperse open areas good for camping.

Past the peaks the trail descends through marshy meadows where its easy to lose your way. Look for the various cairns and posts that bear south and a little west to the junction with Peñas Negras Trail #32.

RED ROCK TRAIL #30:
3 miles   Moderate-Difficult   Elevation: 8,700-9,700 feet

Red Rock Trail is accessed off SH 96 and FR 76 and FR 14. Take SH 96 northeast from Cuba to the town of Gallina, where FR 76 turns southwest (4.4 miles beyond the junction of SH 96 and SH 112). FR 76 then turns southeast for 4.3 miles to the junction with FR 14, which continues south 1.6 miles to the trailhead. This road

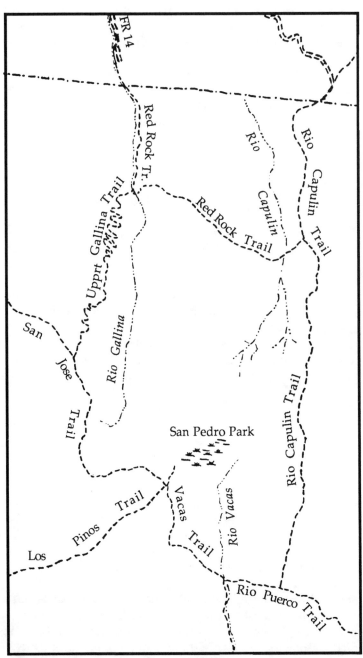

RED ROCK TRAIL #30; UPPER GALLINA TRAIL
#36; RIO CAPULIN TRAIL #31

can be quite muddy and impassable to all but four-wheel drive vehicles in inclement weather.

Red Rock Trail follows the Rio Gallina in a moderate climb through mixed conifer and aspen stands to the junction with Upper Gallina Trail #36 at 1.2 miles. Turn to the left at the junction to continue on Red Rock Trail below the Red Rock Cliffs. The trail is less steep here and continues 2 miles to the Rio Capulin, where good campsites are available. The trail continues another .25 miles to the junction with Rio Capulin Trail #31.

UPPER GALLINA TRAIL #36:
2.6 miles Moderate-Difficult Elevation: 9,000-10,200 feet

An interior wilderness trail, Upper Gallina Trail connects Red Rock Trail #30 and San Jose Trail #33, both accessed off SH 96. The north trailhead intersects the Red Rock Trail 1.2 miles from its trailhead. Follow Trail #36 as it continues south (Red Rock Trail turns east) in a series of switchbacks through dense mixed conifer. Just before the trail tops out on the San Jose Ridge, a spring provides water (and a dug out pool), and cairns help mark the way across the meadows to the junction with San Jose Trail, which leads 2 miles southeast to the Parks, and 4 miles northwest to its trailhead on FR 96.

VEGA REDONDA LOOP (Rio Puerco Trail #385; Vega Redonda Trail #43):
9 miles Moderate Elevation: 9,100-10,000 feet

This is a loop hike through the Vega Redonda (meadow) area, one of the most beautiful of the San Pedro Parks meadows and prime elk habitat. The loop climbs Rio Puerco Trail to Vega Redonda, descends along Vega Redonda Trail, and uses FR 93 as the connecter back to your car. The Vega is a perfect campsite and can also be used as a base camp to explore the trails leading further into the Parks.

To find the trailhead, take SH 96 northeast from SH 44 out of Cuba 23 miles (past the town of Gallina) to FR 103. There is no sign on the highway, but it's an all weather dirt road and a sign is posted as soon as you turn right (south) onto the forest road (FR 76 turns right—west— just past the cattle guard). Follow FR 103

Vega Redonda, typical of the Parks' beautiful meadows

8.7 miles to the junction with FR 93. Turn right (west) on FR 93 and follow it 2.2 miles to the Resumidero Spring area, where a sign says it's .75 miles to the Wilderness boundary, the Vega

Redonda trailhead. Continue on FR 93 2 miles to a dirt road to the right with the sign 385. This is Rio Puerco Trail trailhead. You can park on the side road or along FR 93 by the creek.

Follow the road west alongside the Rio Puerco where it soon narrows to a trail. You cross a tributary of the river and continue along the Rio Puerco through aspen stands and fields of white and purple violets, Rocky Mountain iris, western wallflower, and candytuft. About a .5-mile climb brings you to a large meadow where the trail seems to peter out. Look to your right, and what looks like a road coming down from the top of the meadow is the continuation of the trail, along a tributary of the Rio Puerco. Don't follow the blaze on the tree across the river; this will lead you into a maze of beaver ponds (it is worth a side trip to see all the beaver activity) and felled trees across a trail that eventually leads to a timbering road and to Peñas Negras Trail along a barely discernable route.

Rio Puerco Trail climbs the meadow and crosses back into the trees in a northwesterly direction. The climb steepens as it ascends to the wilderness boundary through mixed conifer forest. Blazes on trees mark the route. The trail levels out just before a descent into a small, lovely meadow full of wild iris. Continue across the meadow to where the trail enters the trees again, and from here it's just a short climb to Vega Redonda.

The first time we ever hiked this trail we saw elk run through the meadow as soon as we came into the clearing. One of the loviest and largest meadows in the wilderness, Vega Redonda is perfect elk habitat as well as perfect human camping habitat. Running water creates marshy areas throughout the Vega, but dry, protected campsites surround the clearing.

Perchas Trail #418 from the south ties in with Rio Puerco Trail at this east end of the meadow. Follow the red posts across the north side of the clearing, along higher ground, to the junction of Rio Puerco Trail and Vega Redonda Trail. A sign here says you've come 3 miles along Rio Puerco Trail from FR 93, although the map indicates it's 3.6 miles (seems like 3 to me) and that it's 3 miles to FR 93 along Vega Redonda Trail. Another sign points the way along Rio Puerco Trail to Oso Creek, at 2 miles; Vega del Oso, 3 miles; and Peñas Negras Trail, 3.25 miles. This is a good place to make a base camp for further exploration into the wilderness along Rio Puerco Trail, which ties in with many of the other wilderness trails and eventually merges with Peñas Negras Trail near the Vacas Trail junction.

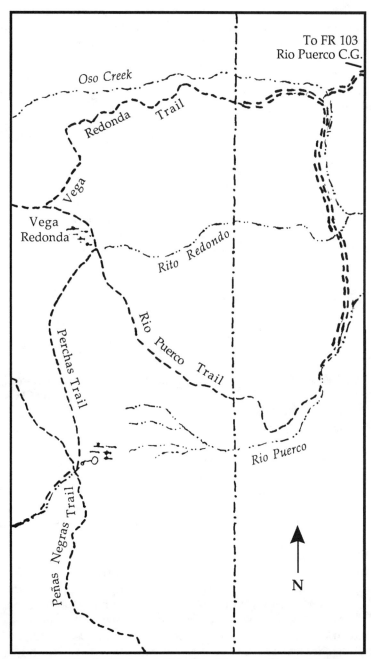

VEGA REDONDA LOOP (Rio Puerco Trail #385;
Vega Redonda Trail #43)

To continue the loop, follow the posts north (right) from the sign along Vega Redonda Trail. Marsh marigold, biscuitroot, and purple violets fill the boggy meadow until the trail enters the trees and then emerges at the spring and beaver pond which signify the headwaters of the Rito Resumidero. The pond is quite large and testifies to the industriousness of the beaver. Vega Redonda continues downhill through mixed conifer forest, through several small meadows, to the banks of the rushing creek. Here the trail turns east across a rocky clearing (follow the posts) and into another clearing called a *vegita* (little meadow). From here the trail descends through the trees to the fence where a spur road leads .75 miles to FR 93 at Resumidero Spring. If you choose to leave a car at this trailhead, or begin your hike here, beware that the road is quite rocky and muddy and requires a high clearance vehicle. If you choose to walk back to your car parked at the Rio Puerco trailhead, the entire loop is 9 miles.

RIO PUERCO TRAIL #385 (Highline Trail):
6 miles   Moderate   Elevation: 8,900-10,300 feet

This trail is a moderately steep climb from the east side of San Pedro Parks to Peñas Negras Trail just east of Vacas Trail. It follows the Rio Puerco along the first part of the route, and water is available all along the hike. To reach the trailhead, follow SH 96 23 miles from the junction of SH 44 (past the town of Gallina) to FR 103. Turn south onto FR 103, and follow it 8.7 miles to the junction of FR 93, which turns west and leads 4.2 miles to the trailhead (beyond the Vega Redondo trailhead) where a dirt road numbered 385 turns right. Park here along the creek or a little ways up the road, which becomes the trail.

The trail climbs through aspen stands along the Rio Puerco for about .5 miles until it turns north and follows a tributary as it climbs through mixed conifer (described in the previous section) to the spectacular Vega Redonda. Perchas Trail ties in with Rio Puerco Trail at this south end of the meadow; Rio Puerco Trail continues across the north side of the clearing to the junction with Vega Redonda Trail, which heads northeast back to FR 93. Rio Puerco Trail continues west across the meadows (follow the posts) and meanders through the spruce-fir forests to Oso Creek, at 2 miles, and Vega del Oso and the junction with Rio Capulin Trail at about 3 miles. Rio Puerco Trail merges with Peñas Negras Trail about .5 miles from Vacas Trail.

BIBLIOGRAPHY

Beard, Sam. *Ski Touring in Northern New Mexico*. Albuquerque: Nordic Press, 1988.

DeBuys, William. *Enchantment and Exploitation*. Albuquerque: University of New Mexico Press, 1985.

Evans, Harry. *50 Hikes in New Mexico*. Pico Rivera, California: Gem Guide Books Company, 1984.

Leopold, Aldo. *Sand County Almanac*. New York: Oxford University Press, 1949.

Lujan, Mabel Dodge. *Winter in Taos*. New York: Harcourt Brace and Company, 1935.

Matthews, Kay. *Cross-Country Skiing in Northern New Mexico*. Placitas: Acequia Madre Press, 1989.

Nichols, John. *If Mountains Die*. New York: Holt Rinehart and Winston, 1982.

Parent, Laurence. *The Hiker's Guide to New Mexico*. Helena, Montana: Falcon Press, 1991.

Pettitt, Roland. *Exploring the Jemez Country*. Los Alamos: Los Alamos Historical Society, 1990.

Santa Fe Group of the Sierra Club. *Day Hikes in the Santa Fe Area*. Santa Fe: 1990.

Southwest Culture and Heritage Association. *Pecos Wilderness*. Albuquerque: 1991.

Ungnade, Herbert E. *Guide to the New Mexico Mountains*. Albuquerque: University of New Mexico Press, 1965.

ALSO AVAILABLE FROM ACEQUIA MADRE PRESS:

Cross-Country Skiing in Northern New Mexico:
An Introduction and Trail Guide, Kay Matthews
96 pages, 5 3/8 x 81/2, maps, illustrations, photos, $7.95 paper

Hiking Trails of the Sandia and Manzano Mountains, Kay
Matthews
86 pages, 5 3/8 x 81/2, maps, photos, $9.95 paper

ACEQUIA MADRE PRESS ORDER FORM
P.O. Box 493,
Placitas, New Mexico 87043
(505) 867-5904

Title	Quantity	Price	Total
Cross-Country Skiing in Northern New Mexico		$7.95	
Hiking Trails of the Sandia and Manzano Mountains		$9.95	
Hiking the Wilderness: A Backpacking Guide to the Wheeler Peak, Pecos, and San Pedro Parks Wilderness Areas		$10.95	
		Subtotal	
		Shipping	$2.50
		Total